WARREN WATSON

PREEMPTS

MASTER POINT PRESS

Master Point Press
214 Merton St. Suite 205
Toronto, Ontario, Canada
M4S 1A6   (647)956-4933

Email:	info@masterpointpress.com
Websites:	www.masterpointpress.com
	www.teachbridge.com
	www.bridgeblogging.com
	www.ebooksbridge.com

Library and Archives Canada Cataloguing in Publication

Title: Preempts / Warren Watson.
Names: Watson, Warren, 1964- author.
Identifiers: Canadiana (print) 20190050373 | Canadiana (ebook) 20190051698 | ISBN 9781771400480
      (softcover) | ISBN 9781554946457 (PDF) | ISBN 9781554946907 (HTML) | ISBN 9781771408899 (Kindle)
Subjects: LCSH: Contract bridge—Bidding.
Classification: LCC GV1282.4 .W38 2019 | DDC 795.41/52—dc23

Canadä | We acknowledge the financial support of the Government of Canada.
Nous reconnaissons l'appui financier du gouvernement du Canada.

Editor	Ray Lee
Copy editor/interior format	Sally Sparrow
Cover design	Olena S. Sullivan/New Mediatrix

1 2 3 4 5 6 7   22 21 20 19
Printed in Canada by Webcom

Preface

What are the best memories from bridge? Certainly they are not all the times the pass card was pulled out — although sometimes 'pass' not 'sorry' is the hardest word (to say). Jumping to the five-level with a huge fit for partner's preempt and no defense, just to watch the opponents squirm, not knowing what to do, could be a candidate. How about sacrificing over a cold slam, and giving the opponents less than their game is worth, not to mention their slam? Probably the worst is having a ton of high cards and seeing the opponents preempt the auction so high that getting to the right spot is near impossible.

Preempts and sacrifices potentially reap the biggest rewards in the game of bridge. Nowadays, bidding systems are so well designed that, in an uncontested auction, most players can get to the correct spot. They are not often so successful in competitive auctions. Taking away as much bidding space as you safely can makes the auction difficult even for an expert player. Grand slams are incredibly hard to bid accurately in a preemptive auction. Even a simple overcall may present a challenge to the opposition, and at the very least, will get partner off to a good lead.

It is important to preempt the opponents, but not partner, as much as you can. When partner has little defense and can raise the preempt, a difficult situation for the opponents has become even more challenging. High-level contracts are not the most common aspect of bridge. That distinction belongs to partscore contracts. However, high-level contracts are certainly the most memorable part of bridge and often the most enjoyable.

This book is divided into three parts:
1) Basic Preempts
2) Advanced Preempts
3) High-Level Competition

This book will make your game of bridge much more successful, and that much more enjoyable. My joy is achieved by passing my knowledge on to you.

Contents

PART 1

BASIC
PREEMPTS

Chapter One

Preempts Work

The examples in this chapter show how preempts make it more difficult for the opponents to get to the correct spot than in an uncontested auction.

Example 1.1 High-level Decisions Involve Guesswork

The following deal was played ninety-four times during an ACBL IMP speedball tourney on BBO (Bridge Base Online). The results on this deal ranged from +920 for 6◊ making to -1700 for 5♣ and 5♡ doubled down seven. Nineteen scores were -500 or worse. The range of defense and declarer play was enormous because, if properly defended, the contracts that make are 4♠ East-West and 4◊ North-South.

Neither vul.

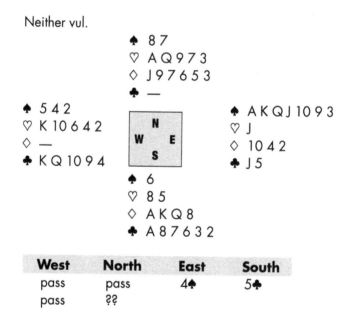

	West	**North**	**East**	**South**
	pass	pass	4♠	5♣
	pass	??		

Because his partner is a passed hand, East should make things difficult for the opponents with a 4♠ opening. As it happens, here he is himself instantly in the correct spot, as he can make at least ten tricks in spades.

This example is very important because East must bid 4♠, not 3♠. Opposite a passed hand, slam is likely out of reach and if he opens 3♠, partner might not recognize he has enough for 4♠ (not the case here). Furthermore, 4♠ is much more an effective impediment to the opponents' bidding. One of the opponents likely has spade shortness and therefore it is probable that the opponents want to bid.

South cannot pass, or the opponents will rob him blind, so he must do something. South tries 5♣ and hopes it is better than defending 4♠. West's second pass is the best bid of the whole sequence. North cannot run from 5♣ if West passes, but if West doubles, North or South may find 5◊. A player should never double the only contract he can defeat, because that may push the opponents to their correct spot. Of course, letting 5♣ play undoubled does not recoup the score 4♠ obtains, but the real point is that 5◊ is cold, and North-South are going to find it hard to bid it after the 4♠ opening.

The bottom line is that preempts add guesswork to the auction. A player can take solace because the next time the opportunity arrives, he will do the same thing to the opponents.

Let's look at what happens when East is in first seat. It's risky to pre-empt to 4♠ because his partner may have a good hand, so he opens 1♠. He then jumps to 4♠, and leaves South with a similar problem to the one we saw before.

West	North	East	South
		1♠	2♣
2♠	pass	4♠	??

Will South find the winning call of 4NT, suggesting diamonds as a possible strain, now? Maybe, but maybe not. The point is to present him with a problem. He won't solve it correctly every time.

Example 1.2 A Preempt Causes the Opponents to Miss a Slam

E-W vul.

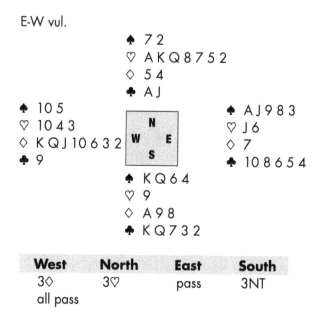

```
                    ♠ 7 2
                    ♡ A K Q 8 7 5 2
                    ◇ 5 4
                    ♣ A J
   ♠ 10 5                          ♠ A J 9 8 3
   ♡ 10 4 3          N             ♡ J 6
   ◇ K Q J 10 6 3 2  W   E         ◇ 7
   ♣ 9                S            ♣ 10 8 6 5 4
                    ♠ K Q 6 4
                    ♡ 9
                    ◇ A 9 8
                    ♣ K Q 7 3 2
```

West	North	East	South
3◇	3♡	pass	3NT
all pass			

I watched self-proclaimed experts on this deal in the BBO partnership bidding room. This is a clear example of how a preempt makes bidding a slam much more difficult. Perhaps 3♡ is something of an underbid, but the point is that the preempt presented North with a problem, and he failed to solve it. Therefore, you must preempt as much as possible.

If West passes initially, it should not be hard to get to slam.

Example 1.3 Bid the Limit of the Hand, Then Be Silent

This hand occurred in the top bracket of a KO at a Victoria regional tournament.

Neither vul.

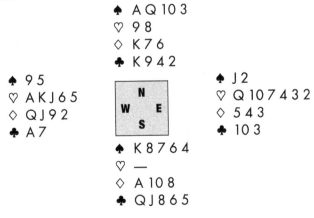

```
              ♠ A Q 10 3
              ♡ 9 8
              ◇ K 7 6
              ♣ K 9 4 2
 ♠ 9 5                          ♠ J 2
 ♡ A K J 6 5          N         ♡ Q 10 7 4 3 2
 ◇ Q J 9 2       W        E     ◇ 5 4 3
 ♣ A 7               S          ♣ 10 3
              ♠ K 8 7 6 4
              ♡ —
              ◇ A 10 8
              ♣ Q J 8 6 5
```

West	North	East	South
		pass	pass
1♡	dbl	5♡	5♠
all pass			

East knows he is eventually going to have to save over 4♠, so it makes sense to bid 5♡ right away. *Make the opponents take the last guess.* South must have thought about a slam because of his heart void, but in the end did not want to risk the game bonus. At the other table, the bidding went as follows.

West	North	East	South
		pass	pass
1♡	dbl	5♡	5♠
pass	pass	6♡	6♠
all pass			

Here East makes the mistake of bidding his hand twice: he should hold his peace having bid 5♡. Our teammate, a very strong player, broke a cardinal rule by making a preempt and then bidding again, and South was given a second chance to make the winning bid. Here, 5♡ doubled is down three for -500 when the opponents can get 980. That is not bad as it is a loss of 1

IMP compared to 480. At matchpoints and equal vulnerability, East will be more conservative, and probably bids only 4♡. At IMPs, 5♡ is a very good bid, taking away a lot of room, including ace-asking bids; it is as equally good as the 6♡ bid is bad.

Example 1.4 Did Choosing Not to Preempt Give Away an Advantage?

The following was the last board of the last match of the Sunday team game in a Vernon sectional.

Both vul.

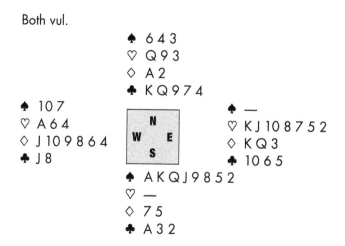

```
              ♠ 6 4 3
              ♡ Q 9 3
              ◊ A 2
              ♣ K Q 9 7 4
   ♠ 10 7                      ♠ —
   ♡ A 6 4         N           ♡ K J 10 8 7 5 2
   ◊ J 10 9 8 6 4  W   E       ◊ K Q 3
   ♣ J 8               S       ♣ 10 6 5
              ♠ A K Q J 9 8 5 2
              ♡ —
              ◊ 7 5
              ♣ A 3 2
```

At our table, the bidding went:

West	North	East	South
	pass	3♡	4♠
5♡	dbl	pass	5♠
all pass			

At the other table, East passed because of his spade void, and the bidding went:

West	North	East	South
	pass	pass	2♣
pass	3♣	3♡	3♠
4♡	4♠	5♡	6♠
all pass			

We gained 13 IMPs for +1460 versus +710. After the preempt, the opponents would have been gambling to bid 7♠, and can never rightfully get there. Personally, I would not preempt with a void and a maximum, so will the opponents find the grand against me? No, because after an initial pass I would bid 4♡, not 3♡, over 3♣. Bidding 4♡ takes away Exclusion Blackwood, which must be a jump, and 5♡ takes away 4NT. However, 5♡ cannot be bid unilaterally. A jump to 5♡ is like a sitting duck, as the opponents almost always sit for a double. Do people bid grands at teams? Of course they do if thirteen tricks are there, because team games reward good bridge.

Example 1.5   A Preempt Induces a Mistake

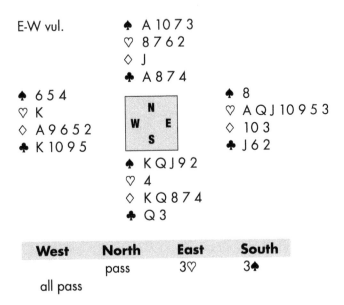

E-W vul.

```
              ♠ A 10 7 3
              ♡ 8 7 6 2
              ◇ J
              ♣ A 8 7 4
♠ 6 5 4                        ♠ 8
♡ K                            ♡ A Q J 10 9 5 3
◇ A 9 6 5 2      N             ◇ 10 3
♣ K 10 9 5     W   E           ♣ J 6 2
                 S
              ♠ K Q J 9 2
              ♡ 4
              ◇ K Q 8 7 4
              ♣ Q 3
```

West	North	East	South
	pass	3♡	3♠
all pass			

This example occurred during an ACBL IMP speedball tourney on BBO. East has a minimum vulnerable preempt, but he has an excellent suit with good intermediates and spade shortness. There is no doubt that East was correct to evaluate his hand as worth a vulnerable 3♡ because preempts can induce a mistake. West has enough that 4♡ makes, but cannot bid it because it would push the opponents to a making 4♠ contract.

In an unimpeded auction, South will open 1♠ and accept partner's limit raise for +420. East preempts, and North mistakenly decides to pass 3♠. Preempts take a player out of his comfort zone.

Example 1.6 Cool Grand Luke

Neither vul.

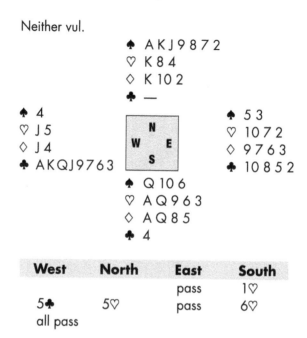

	West	North	East	South
			pass	1♡
	5♣	5♡	pass	6♡
	all pass			

This deal occurred at matchpoints. West has a 12-count and an eight-card suit, but his partner is a passed hand, and he is extremely short in the majors. Making 3NT is well-nigh impossible opposite a passed hand so the preempt makes sense. South, after hearing 5♡, is pretty sure a small slam is there, and North suspects a grand may be possible, but bidding a grand would be a gamble. South settles for a small slam, which is usually a decent score, while going down in a grand is usually a zero.

Suppose, on a different layout, East-West stay out of the auction. Clearly, without a preempt a grand can be bid, although it may not be reached. However, when there is a preempt it often does not matter what slam bidding is theoretically possible. The examples in this chapter illustrate how preempts compromise the bidding; most players will not gamble, but bid only what they can be reasonably sure of making. However, if you have been put in this situation, remember to return the favor and do the same to the opponents when you can. Disciplined preempts, as discussed in the next chapter, allow partner to do the right thing when he has high cards.

Example 1.7 Preempting One's Own Side

This happened at the Unit 574, Kootenay, BC, Christmas party. Sitting West, I had a very pleasant partner..

Neither vul.

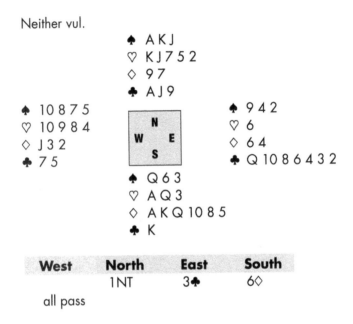

```
                  ♠ A K J
                  ♡ K J 7 5 2
                  ◊ 9 7
                  ♣ A J 9
  ♠ 10 8 7 5                      ♠ 9 4 2
  ♡ 10 9 8 4        N            ♡ 6
  ◊ J 3 2        W     E         ◊ 6 4
  ♣ 7 5             S            ♣ Q 10 8 6 4 3 2
                  ♠ Q 6 3
                  ♡ A Q 3
                  ◊ A K Q 10 8 5
                  ♣ K
```

West	North	East	South
	1NT	3♣	6◊
all pass			

East made an undisciplined preempt, and actually took credit for keeping South out of the proper slam. South asked North why he didn't correct to 6NT. North's reply was, 'I do not do that.' Now, North-South are on the same team. 'Mutiny on the Bounty' is meant for the big screen not for the bridge table. You should not sign off in a small slam unless you are certain a grand cannot make. The wrong slam bid, 6◊, took away all the space needed for a possible good bidding sequence. The real preempt was 6◊ not 3♣.

West	North	East	South
	1NT	3♣	4♣
pass	4♡	pass	4NT
pass	5◊	pass	5NT
pass	6♣	pass	7NT
all pass			

This is one sequence that could get them to 7NT. The cuebid forces to game, and the resulting auction is fairly straightforward.

Example 1.8 A Preempt 'Bid to Make'

Both vul.

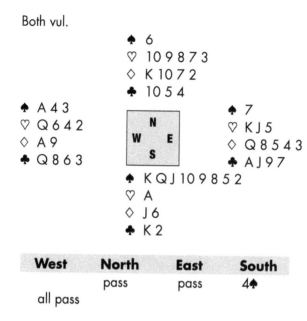

```
              ♠ 6
              ♡ 10 9 8 7 3
              ◇ K 10 7 2
              ♣ 10 5 4
  ♠ A 4 3              ♠ 7
  ♡ Q 6 4 2     N       ♡ K J 5
  ◇ A 9      W     E    ◇ Q 8 5 4 3
  ♣ Q 8 6 3     S       ♣ A J 9 7
              ♠ K Q J 10 9 8 5 2
              ♡ A
              ◇ J 6
              ♣ K 2
```

West	North	East	South
	pass	pass	4♠
all pass			

This board came up in an ACBL BBO speedball tourney. Out of ninety-seven tables, thirty played in 4♠ doubled making, for a gain of 5.75 IMPs. Undoubled, it was +1.92 IMPs. Five East-West pairs tried club sacrifices that were fairly successful, presenting North-South with a loss of 4 IMPs or so. The eight pairs not in game incurred a loss of 6.25 IMPs. Eighteen pairs went down in a spade contract for a loss of 9.46 IMPs or 10.95 IMPs if doubled.

Because partner is a passed hand, this is clearly a 4♠ opening. This is not exactly a preempt, but it is designed to keep the opposition quiet. One opponent likely has spade shortness, and it is quite possible that he cannot bid over 4♠ when he certainly would over 1♠. In addition, 4♠ is bid to make because partner will never know he has the small amount necessary for you to make game. Just the ♣A is enough to guarantee it, for example. Even if North has only the ◇K, there is at least a play for 4♠. This preempt worked constructively for the preempting side.

Example 1.9   A Delayed Preempt Works

N-S vul.

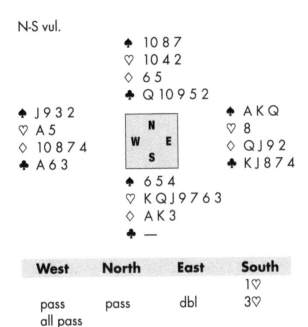

West	North	East	South
			1♡
pass	pass	dbl	3♡
all pass			

This is another example of a preempt that worked, but the bidding did not start with a preempt. South opened 1♡ because he was too strong for a preempt, but when his partner passed, he knew game was out of reach. Therefore, he could preempt to prevent the opponents from finding their correct spot.

Out of 97 pairs in an ACBL BBO speedball tourney, three East-West pairs made 3♣ and four made +140 in spades. Only a few made +140 North-South because most were pushed to 4♡ down one. However, while it is fairly easy for West to bid at the one- or two-level, it's not so clear to come in over 3♡.

Chapter Two

Disciplined Preempts

Preempts should be made as much as possible to cause the opponents to misstep in the bidding. After an undisciplined preempt, the partner of the preemptor won't go wrong when he has no high cards. However, *disciplined preempts must be the norm in first or second seat* in case partner has a good hand — otherwise you are simply taking away your own bidding space.

Example 2.1   It's a Trap! May the Fourth Be With You!

This is the first example I use in my high-level bidding workshop. It gives me an idea of how my students preempt.

N-S vul.

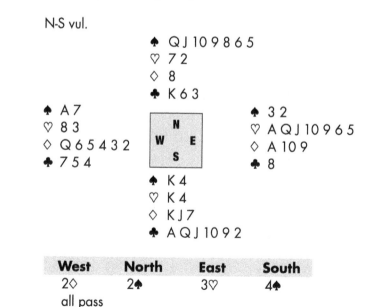

a.

	West	**North**	**East**	**South**
	2◊	2♠	3♡	4♠
	all pass			

b.

West	North	East	South
pass	3♠	4♡	4♠
all pass			

c.

West	North	East	South
pass	pass	1♡	1NT
pass	4♡	pass	4♠
all pass			

The question I ask them, is 'Which auction is correct?'

The answer I want is, 'None of the above'.

The first auction has many flaws. West has too poor a suit to open 2◊, and if he does, North is too weak to overcall. He should not preempt — never preempt over a preempt — so bidding 3♠ is out. East, with a semi-solid suit and a diamond fit, should clearly bid 4♡ over 2♠. And if North has a real 2♠ overcall, vulnerable, South should be looking for slam.

In the second auction, when West passes, North has a good enough suit to preempt but too weak a hand at this vulnerability. I find that most of my students, however, open 3♠ sitting North.

Therefore, two passes should come around to East, but that does not make auction (c) correct. What is East doing bidding only 1♡? That is the bid you make on these cards in first or second seat, but not in third seat when partner is a passed hand at favorable vulnerability. Even 3♡ is not the correct bid, as it leaves the opponents too much bidding room.

West	North	East	South
pass	pass	3♡	4♣
pass	4♠	all pass	

East can prevent the opponents finding their correct contract because of his good long suit. He knows that slam is impossible opposite a passed hand so 4♡ is his best opening bid. It is either going to make or be a good obstruction to the opponents. Here is the correct auction:

West	North	East	South
pass	pass	4♡	5♣
all pass			

As we have seen, North will bid 4♠ over 4♣, a game over a partscore any-time, but on this deal the five-level is too high. Notice that East has bid his hand at his first turn, and must hold his peace thereafter. He must allow the preempt to do its work. He should take his positive score and not bid again over 5♣. East prevents North-South from getting to the correct contract at little risk — here, 4♡ doubled is only down one. In practice, North-South cannot double 4♡ even if they want to: a direct double by South would be for takeout (a direct double is penalty only if the opening is 4♠ or higher). That is a pretty common treatment. So South was given an unsolvable problem by East, and he just has to hope that he can do the same to East sometime.

SUIT QUALITY

If a player preempts in clubs, the main strength of his hand is in clubs. A descriptive bid has been made. He has little outside defense and has a good-enough suit (including some top honors) to draw trumps, especially if he ends up playing doubled. He should also have good-enough intermediates to handle bad splits. When you end up doubled, it is often because of a bad trump split. Furthermore, the preempt is suggesting a sacrifice to partner who may have good support and little defense, not unlike the double of any shortness bid (see examples 10.7 and 11.1). For example, the suit could look like the following:

$$A\,J\,10\,5\,4\,3\,2 \qquad A\,Q\,8\,7\,6\,5\,2 \qquad A\,K\,8\,7\,6\,3\,2$$

But not:

$$A\,J\,9\,5\,4\,3\,2 \qquad A\,10\,9\,8\,7\,6\,5 \qquad A\,8\,7\,6\,4\,3\,2$$

I could list several more examples, but instead the following rule of thumb should be used. The suit should have:

Two of the top three honors
or
Three of the top five honors

Example 2.2 Starting the Auction Above the Opponents' Optimum Contract

Both vul.

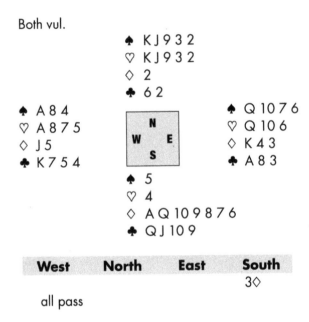

```
               ♠ K J 9 3 2
               ♡ K J 9 3 2
               ◇ 2
               ♣ 6 2
♠ A 8 4                          ♠ Q 10 7 6
♡ A 8 7 5          N             ♡ Q 10 6
◇ J 5          W       E         ◇ K 4 3
♣ K 7 5 4          S             ♣ A 8 3
               ♠ 5
               ♡ 4
               ◇ A Q 10 9 8 7 6
               ♣ Q J 10 9
```

West	North	East	South
			3◇

all pass

South has a meaty preempt as expected when vulnerable, and the extreme shortness in the majors makes a preempt absolutely necessary. West does not have the strength to enter the auction, and East does not have good enough shape to balance, so the auction ends there.

How South fares in 3◇ here will depend on how he plays the trump suit. There are no dummy entries, so if the missing honors are in the same hand (and not doubleton), nothing can be done to prevent two diamond losers. In this situation, I always arbitrarily play for the jack to be doubleton. I cash the ◇A and then play the ◇Q, ideally smothering the jack. In the long run, this will be right about half the time. Here South will lose one spade, one heart, one diamond and two clubs for down one and minus 100.

Without the preempt, East or West could end up in a notrump partscore, and likely making at least +120. However, most Souths will preempt, and a loss of 100 will not be a bad score because some will play for the king to be doubleton and go down two.

Example 2.3 Watch the Intermediate Cards

Neither vul.

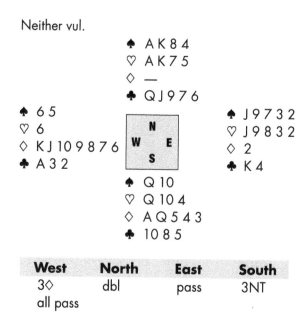

	♠ A K 8 4	
	♡ A K 7 5	
	◊ —	
	♣ Q J 9 7 6	
♠ 6 5		♠ J 9 7 3 2
♡ 6		♡ J 9 8 3 2
◊ K J 10 9 8 7 6		◊ 2
♣ A 3 2		♣ K 4
	♠ Q 10	
	♡ Q 10 4	
	◊ A Q 5 4 3	
	♣ 10 8 5	

West	North	East	South
3◊	dbl	pass	3NT
all pass			

West has a solid preempt, but on this layout the opponents can get to 3NT and make it. West should lead a diamond anyway, as that will work if East can get in early and has a second diamond to lead through. Not this time. Some pretty good players have the rule that they never preempt with an outside ace. I do not have that rule, but holding outside honors often means that the preempt suit is too poor to preempt, as shown in this next deal:

Neither vul.

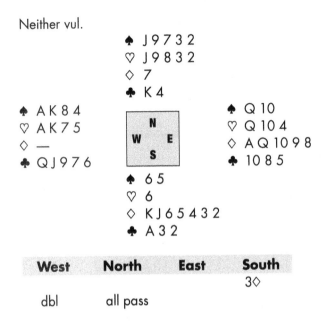

♠	J 9 7 3 2
♡	J 9 8 3 2
◊	7
♣	K 4

♠ A K 8 4   ♠ Q 10
♡ A K 7 5   ♡ Q 10 4
◊ —   ◊ A Q 10 9 8
♣ Q J 9 7 6   ♣ 10 8 5

♠ 6 5
♡ 6
◊ K J 6 5 4 3 2
♣ A 3 2

West	North	East	South
			3◊
dbl	all pass		

It is the quality of suit intermediates that often make or break a preempt that includes an outside ace. This hand begs the question, 'Cannot South see his small diamonds?', because East can certainly see his large diamonds. East-West are entitled to at least +430 in 3NT, but may get +460 if South leads a diamond, and they will rack up +500 or more if South preempts. Reverse the East-West hands and the carnage is even greater.

Hand Strength

Not only must a preempt have a good suit to draw trumps and good intermediates to withstand a bad break, it should fall into a particular point range depending on the vulnerability. A preempt is typically:

| 5-9 HCP | not vulnerable |
| 7-10 HCP | vulnerable |

The weaker hands will have all of their high cards in the trump suit. The stronger hands will not be good enough to make game opposite a minimum opening from partner. This makes a lot of two-suited hands (6-4 or better) too strong to open as a preempt. A two-suited preempt and one containing a void will be at the low end of the point range.

Example 2.4   A Better One-level Opener than a Preempt

Both vul.

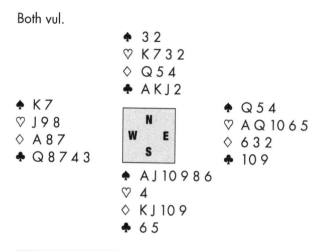

West	North	East	South
			1♠
pass	2♣	pass	2◊
pass	2NT	pass	3♠
pass	4♠	all pass	

Two-suited hands are often a problem to bid. Many partners may object to a 9-HCP opener, but a 1♠ opening is far superior to 2♠ in this example. Even a pass is better than 2♠ (perhaps a pass would be preferred by a partner who vehemently objects to 1♠).

By the way, South is not trying to pull a fast one, he just recognizes the potential of the hand, and he does not need particularly good support from his partner. Can you see the good intermediates and touching cards in South's hand? He certainly can. By contrast, the following hand is an easy pass:

♠ A J 5 4 3 2   ♡ 4   ◊ K J 3 2   ♣ 6 5

On this layout, South will lose one spade, one heart and one diamond for +620. *An opener opposite an opener will make game.* Since North has a minimum-range opener, it follows that South has the equivalent to an opening hand.

Example 2.5 Preempts Do Not Include a Four-card Major

Both vul.

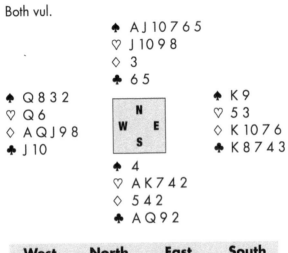

	West	North	East	South
		pass	pass	1♡
	pass	2♣*	pass	2◇
	pass	4♡	all pass	

In first or second seat, a preempt should not include a void or a four-card major as this could also make the hand a very good dummy.

Here, North passes ahead of partner because of the side four-card major in a hand that would otherwise open a weak 2♠. South opens 1♡, and North can raise hearts in whatever way their agreements allow. Here North uses Reverse Drury, and raises to 4♡ once he knows South has a real opener. South will make 4♡ on this layout, but if North opens 2♠ that is where they will play.

HOW HIGH?

The Length Method
Suit length is the most commonly used and easiest indicator for deciding how high to preempt. The cards are simply counted.

6	weak two
7	weak three
8	weak four
9	weak five

This is independent of vulnerability. However, if you are vulnerable, judgment may dictate a pass instead of a preempt. You will pass and come in later with a simple overcall if possible. The length rule is strictly obeyed with preempts made in first or second seat ahead of partner. A weak two is not made with seven cards, for example. I would rather not see rules broken, but if this rule is going to be broken, it is better to do it with a good suit and good intermediates. *Bridge is all about knowing when the rules can be broken.*

Example 2.6 Simple as ABC Not 123

At favorable vulnerability in first or second seat, what do you bid with these hands, considering the length rule?

a)	♠ 3 2 ♡ K Q 10 9 8 7 ◇ Q 10 6 ♣ 3 2	2♡
b)	♠ K Q 10 9 8 7 ♡ 3 2 ◇ 10 9 6 ♣ 3 2	2♠
c)	♠ 7 ♡ 3 2 ◇ 10 9 6 ♣ K Q 10 9 8 7 6	3♣
d)	♠ 7 ♡ K 2 ◇ 10 9 6 ♣ K Q 10 9 8 7 6	3♣
e)	♠ 7 ♡ 2 ◇ Q 10 2 ♣ K Q J 10 9 8 7 6	4♣
f)	♠ 7 ♡ 2 ◇ K 10 ♣ K Q J 10 9 8 7 6 5	5♣
g)	♠ 7 ♡ 2 ◇ 10 2 ♣ K Q J 10 9 8 7 6 5	5♣

If you are vulnerable, cases (b) and (c) are passes and case (g) is better dialed back one level rather than giving up on the hand with a pass. If case (g) is opened 4♣ vulnerable, the opponents may still be prevented from getting to the correct spot without being offered too much from the contract going down doubled. The case for caution is greatest at unfavorable vulnerability and least at favorable vulnerability. Equal vulnerability is in the middle. The rules of 123 and 234 (see page 40) give more consideration to this, while the length rule is essentially binary, on or off.

However, with the length rule, being vulnerable is given the most consideration because down two vulnerable undoubled or down one doubled is -200, a disastrous matchpoint score compared to most partscores. Down two or three, doubled and vulnerable, gives the opponents more than their games, not vulnerable and vulnerable respectively.

The Modified Length Method

The common exception to the length rule of preempts is opening 3♣ with only a six-card suit. This is relatively common as there is no weak two in clubs available for most natural systems. If you do this in first or second seat, you should have two cards or fewer in each side major. I have the same rule for a five-card weak two. Furthermore, I may pretend a hand with a singleton is a hand with one extra trump solely for the purpose of the length rule of preempts.

You may want to extend this to 3◊ openings if 2◊ is not used as weak. However, I personally prefer to play a weak 2◊ because I think that removing the opponents' bidding room is important when weak. In my experience, a weak two comes up more frequently than hands that fit the other uses of 2◊ — hands which can mostly be bid naturally anyway, except perhaps a strong 4-4-4-1 hand. So yes, hands like:

$$♠AKJ3 \quad ♡AJ53 \quad ◊AKJ4 \quad ♣J$$

may be bid more accurately with a Roman 2◊, but it will be very infrequent. Treat this as a 1◊ opening, and then 2◊ can be used for the much more common weak two hands.

Example 2.7 The Length Rule is Not Rigid

At favorable vulnerability in first or second seat, what do you bid with the following using the modified length rule of preempts?

a)   ♠32 ♡87 ◊K62 ♣KJ10982
b)   ♠932 ♡87 ◊Q6 ♣KJ10982
c)   ♠32 ♡87 ◊KQJ109 ♣10982
d)   ♠63 ♡873 ◊KQJ109 ♣542
e)   ♠2 ♡KQJ98 ◊8762 ♣752
f)   ♠2 ♡KQJ987 ◊8762 ♣32
g)   ♠982 ♡KQJ98 ◊87 ♣762
h)   ♠KQJ98 ♡10987 ◊87 ♣87

I would not be surprised if you currently do not preempt as recommended above with (c), (e) and (f). Perhaps, since you are reading this book, you can change.

(a) 3♣. This hand has a doubleton (or less) in each major, and the club suit is a fine suit. It is not the best suit from which to lead, but it is certainly a suit you want partner to lead.

(b) Pass. This is not a six-card three-level preempt because of the three spades, the second flaw. It is not a coincidence in these examples that the intermediate cards are good. A six-card three-level preempt is the first flaw. Take away the good intermediates and there would be a third flaw. Bids with two or more flaws are not made.

(c) 2◊. You have a doubleton in each major and a superb five-card diamond suit. At the very least, a diamond lead is needed.

(d) Pass. This hand has a five-card suit for a weak two. That is the first flaw. The second flaw, like in (b), is a three-card major.

(e) 2♡. This should be opened in first or second seat as 2♡ because the singleton makes the hearts feel like a six-card suit. Not to mention that the opponents may have lots of spades.

(f) 3♡. This is clearly a 3♡ opening if partner is a passed hand. However, if preempting ahead of partner, a player tries to keep his opening consistent with the length rule except when the unbid majors are very short. Here there is a singleton spade. The exception also applies to a really good five-card weak two — like (c) and (e) — with two cards or fewer in any unbid major.

(g) Pass. This hand clearly has a good five-card suit, and the defense would be easier if partner can lead it, however three-card spade support is the second flaw.

(h) Pass. This hand includes an outside four-card major, which would also be a flaw even if the spade suit were the proper length.

The Five-Card Weak Two

As you have seen in examples (c) and (e) above, I do not follow the rule that a weak two must always be six cards. No, it cannot be seven cards in first or second seat; however, it can be five cards. Nevertheless, a five-card weak two must meet the following criteria:

- A strong suit such as AKJ107, KQJ98, etc., because wanting the suit led is not even a question.
- Two cards or fewer in any unbid major.
- Ideally 5-4 shape (four cards in a minor, not a major).

In third seat, the criteria are reduced to the following:

- A reasonable suit with good intermediate cards, such as AJ987, AQ1087, etc.

Example 2.8 A Two-suited Preempt when Minimum

E-W vul.

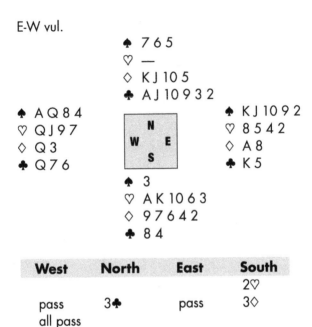

| ♠ 7 6 5 |
| ♡ — |
| ◊ K J 10 5 |
| ♣ A J 10 9 3 2 |

♠ A Q 8 4   ♠ K J 10 9 2
♡ Q J 9 7   ♡ 8 5 4 2
◊ Q 3   ◊ A 8
♣ Q 7 6   ♣ K 5

♠ 3
♡ A K 10 6 3
◊ 9 7 6 4 2
♣ 8 4

West	North	East	South
			2♡
pass	3♣	pass	3◊
all pass			

This deal occurred during an ACBL matchpoint speedball tourney on BBO. South preempted on a very good five-card suit because he was short in the other major. West cannot double with his shape, and is too weak for 2NT. North bid 3♣, forcing one round. South then bid 3◊, and to his surprise, his partner passed.

The board was played forty times, and 3◊ plus one was worth 90.54%. Three East-West pairs were in 4♠ making, and 4♠ went down one sixteen times. East-West were doubled in an excessive number of hearts for a big number three times.

Example 2.9   A Singleton Somewhere

E-W vul.

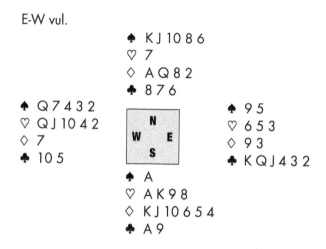

♠ K J 10 8 6
♥ 7
♦ A Q 8 2
♣ 8 7 6

♠ Q 7 4 3 2
♥ Q J 10 4 2
♦ 7
♣ 10 5

♠ 9 5
♥ 6 5 3
♦ 9 3
♣ K Q J 4 3 2

♠ A
♥ A K 9 8
♦ K J 10 6 5 4
♣ A 9

West	North	East	South
	2♠	pass	3◇
pass	4♡	pass	4NT
pass	5♣	dbl	5♡
pass	5♠	pass	7◇
all pass			

This is a fictitious deal based on one that occurred in an ACBL BBO speed-ball IMP tourney. In the actual game, North had two hearts and three diamonds, and North erred by not showing diamond support. North-South played in 3NT for a gain of 1.28 IMPs. Ten out of 104 pairs were in small slam, and one actually bid 7◇. Getting to 6◇ was worth +11.77 IMPs.

I changed the deal because I love splinters, which are highly effective. In fact, Mike Lawrence states, in his book, *Hand Evaluation*, that a splinter is often more effective than extensive cuebidding.

Furthermore, five-card weak twos are better with a singleton somewhere. Could North open 1♠? It's borderline, but for me, North's heart shortness solidifies it as a weak two.

Furthermore, 3NT is clearly wrong with a singleton heart. In my example auction, 3◇ is forcing for one round, and North splinters to show heart shortness and four-card diamond support. After that, 5♣ is one key-card, 5♡ is asking for the ◇Q and 5♠ says, 'Yes, with the ♠K.' (Note that 5◇ cannot ask for the queen because it is to play.)

THE FIVE-CARD WEAK THREE

Example 2.10 The Road to Bridge Hell is Paved with Good Intentions

I am going straight to (bridge) hell for this one.

E-W vul.

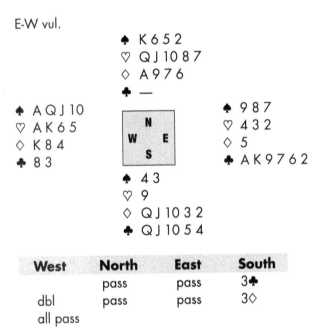

	♠ K 6 5 2
	♡ Q J 10 8 7
	◊ A 9 7 6
	♣ —

♠ A Q J 10		♠ 9 8 7
♡ A K 6 5	N	♡ 4 3 2
◊ K 8 4	W E	◊ 5
♣ 8 3	S	♣ A K 9 7 6 2

	♠ 4 3
	♡ 9
	◊ Q J 10 3 2
	♣ Q J 10 5 4

West	North	East	South
	pass	pass	3♣
dbl	pass	pass	3◊
all pass			

At favorable vulnerability, when partner is a passed hand, and a player is 5-5 in the minors, he should put the pressure on the opponents by opening 3♣ with this shape. The idea is that if the takeout double gets passed, he can run to 3◊.

As it happens, on this deal South will make 3◊ for +110, which is just as well since East-West have no real place to play. However, the principle remains: put pressure on the opponents every chance you get.

First or Second Seat

In first or second seat, preempts must be disciplined in case partner has a good hand. In first seat, there is a 33% chance of preempting partner, and in second seat, there is a 50% chance you are preempting partner. Therefore, preempts in second seat are the most disciplined and should never vary. In third seat, when partner has passed, rules can be relaxed except for general hand strength and wanting the preempt suit led. In fourth seat, a jump is no longer a preempt, because passing keeps the opponents from bidding.

Third Seat Preempts

I once heard the opponents comment on a five-card weak two that a player had made in third seat, and the preemptor's partner, an expert, scoffed, 'When is it not a five-card suit?' Yes, it can certainly be a reasonable five-card suit with good intermediates. Weak twos put pressure on the opponents to do the right thing, and they often do not.

Yes, I repeat, *most people can bid quite nicely in an unimpeded auction.* Not only may a third-seat weak two be five cards, a third-seat preempt can have opening-bid values if game is known to be out of reach across from a passed hand. This is bid to make and to discourage the opponents from finding their fit, particularly in an unbid major.

Example 2.11 A Third-seat Weak Two

This is an example of when *not* to open a five-card weak two in third seat.

Neither vul.

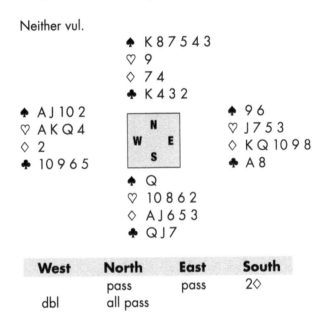

♠	K 8 7 5 4 3
♡	9
◊	7 4
♣	K 4 3 2

♠ A J 10 2
♡ A K Q 4
◊ 2
♣ 10 9 6 5

♠ 9 6
♡ J 7 5 3
◊ K Q 10 9 8
♣ A 8

♠ Q
♡ 10 8 6 2
◊ A J 6 5 3
♣ Q J 7

West	North	East	South
	pass	pass	2◊
dbl	all pass		

Yes, it is perfectly alright and common to make a five-card weak two in third seat, but South's hand has two warning signs. First of all, the suit has no intermediates: the ◊7 should be a good contribution from dummy, but it is not. The second warning sign is the wasted spade honor. This is a minor sign, but preempts often cause the opponents to overbid, and any wasted honor will not pull its weight on defense and might let the opponents scrape home in an otherwise poor contract.

Here, 2◊ doubled was set two for a loss of 300 and a loss of 4 IMPs in an ACBL Speedball event on BBO. In fact, it could have been a lot worse — best defense holds declarer to four tricks. Yes, North could have run to 2♠, but it is usually best not to try to save partner, especially by running to a suit in which West has implied length. The quality of East's diamond suit, not South's, is appropriate for a third-seat five-card weak two.

Example 2.12 A Third-seat Preempt May Not Be Weak

E-W vul.

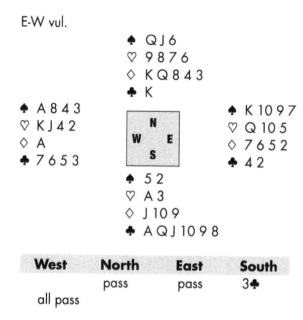

```
                  ♠ Q J 6
                  ♡ 9 8 7 6
                  ◇ K Q 8 4 3
                  ♣ K
  ♠ A 8 4 3                        ♠ K 10 9 7
  ♡ K J 4 2          N             ♡ Q 10 5
  ◇ A            W       E         ◇ 7 6 5 2
  ♣ 7 6 5 3          S             ♣ 4 2
                  ♠ 5 2
                  ♡ A 3
                  ◇ J 10 9
                  ♣ A Q J 10 9 8
```

West	North	East	South
	pass	pass	3♣
all pass			

It was Terence Reese who once wrote, 'A preempt that is known to be weak is a blunt sword.' In third seat, anything goes, and that means that you can preempt on a strong hand as well as a weak one. Here, South knows that game is very likely out of reach opposite a passed hand, and also that the opponents probably have a good major-suit fit. Whether they do or not, South lets them try to find it starting at the three-level. On this deal, South gets +110 instead of losing 140 as he would if East-West were allowed to play in spades.

Example 2.13 A Third-seat Preempt May Be Bid to Make

Both vul.

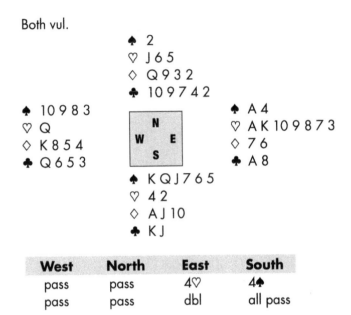

♠	2
♡	J 6 5
◇	Q 9 3 2
♣	10 9 7 4 2

West	North	East	South
pass	pass	4♡	4♠
pass	pass	dbl	all pass

East figures that slam is out of the picture opposite a passed partner and that 4♡ has a good chance of making. Furthermore, he wants to make it difficult for the opponents to find their fit. South, assuming 4♡ was weak and with a good hand himself, tries 4♠. When East doubles, everybody at the table knows that East was bidding to make with lots of meat to his bid. On best defense, 4♠ doubled goes down four for +1100 instead of just +620.

Example 2.14 A Strange Animal

N-S vul.

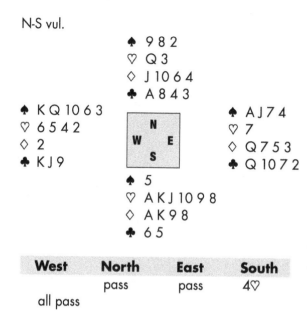

	North	East	South
West	**North**	**East**	**South**
	pass	pass	4♡
all pass			

A third-seat preempt really is a strange animal. As shown in the last example, game can be bid with full expectation of making if slam is known to be out of reach opposite a passed hand. Partner often has around 8 HCP. And if the opponents step into this auction, a double often follows. Sometimes, as here, the opponents will not know how to enter the auction even though they too can make game.

If South opens 1♡ instead, West has a routine 1♠ overcall, and now both sides have found their fit. At this vulnerability, East-West may find a cheap save in 4♠ doubled, or push their opponents too high.

Fourth-seat Preempts

Fourth-seat preempts are, of course, a contradiction in terms. Preempts attempt to stop the opponents from bidding accurately, and yet at the same time they are descriptive bids that allow partner to do the right thing if he has some values. When the auction comes to a player in fourth seat after three passes, the best way to stop the opponents from bidding is to pass, not to make a standard preempt.

So a preempt in fourth seat not only shows the appropriate length but also enough high cards to make what you have bid opposite a probable 7 or 8 points from partner. Furthermore, unless you are opening 4♡ or higher, game must be deemed to be out of reach opposite a passed hand. I would say the range is a good 9 HCP to 13 HCP. With anything less than a full opener, your hand should include four or more spades for defensive purposes — you are giving the opponents one more chance to bid, and it would be disastrous if they were to outbid you to a making spade contract.

Example 2.15 Fourth-seat Preempts Should Be Equivalent to an Opener

E-W vul.

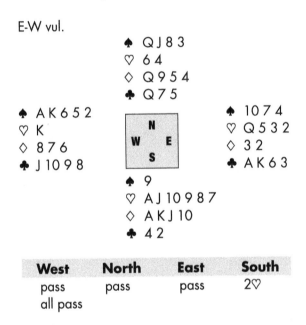

North
♠ Q J 8 3
♡ 6 4
◇ Q 9 5 4
♣ Q 7 5

West
♠ A K 6 5 2
♡ K
◇ 8 7 6
♣ J 10 9 8

East
♠ 10 7 4
♡ Q 5 3 2
◇ 3 2
♣ A K 6 3

South
♠ 9
♡ A J 10 9 8 7
◇ A K J 10
♣ 4 2

West	North	East	South
pass	pass	pass	2♡
all pass			

South could pass the auction out and hope for a decent score because he does not have spades. However, he decides to open such an offense-oriented hand. If he opens 1♡, there is a much greater risk of a 1♠ over-call. South opens 2♡, and the vulnerability keeps the opponents out of the auction. West has a wasted honor, and East cannot handle a diamond response to a double.

Here, South will lose one spade, one heart, no diamonds and two clubs for +140. East-West can make 110 in either 3♣ or 2♠. If East-West do enter the fight, they may stumble into 3♠ doubled for -200. Bidding 3♣ pushes South into a making 3♡ contract at the high risk of a 3♠ bid. So it turns out South does much better to open than to pass the auction out.

PREEMPTING BY LOSERS

I read Ron Klinger's *The Modern Losing Trick Count* when I started playing duplicate. It is one of the most important bridge books I have read. You may glean some of my other favorites from references in this book.

To determine how many losers a hand has, count:

- the missing top three honors (the ace, king and queen) in any suit three cards or longer,
- the missing top two honors (the ace and king) in a two-card suit, and
- the missing top honor (the ace) in a one-card suit.

These holdings all count as three losers, the maximum one suit can have:

xxx, xxxx, xxxxx, etc.

These are two losers:

xx, Jx, Qx, Axx, Kxx, Qxx, Axxx, Kxxx, Qxxx, Axxxx,etc.

These are one loser:

x, Ax, Kx, AQ, KQ, AKx, AQx, KQx, AKxx, AQxx, KQxx, AKxxx, etc.

These are zero losers:

void, A, AK, AKQ, AKQx, AKQxx, AKQxxx, etc.

Using the Losing Trick Count (LTC), the losers in both hands are counted, and the total is subtracted from twenty-four to give a rough estimate of the number of tricks possible. Klinger maintains that the LTC is not a replacement for high-card points, just an adjunct. He uses it for trump contracts with a nine-card fit or better and even with a good eight-card fit.

Example 2.16 Losing Trick Count

Both vulnerable, you, as South, pick up the following hand:

$$\spadesuit A Q 10 5 4 3 \quad \heartsuit A K 7 4 \quad \diamondsuit A K \quad \clubsuit 3$$

You open 1♠ and partner raises to 2♠. What do you bid?

You have three losers. A minimum opener is seven losers, an invitational hand is eight losers and a simple raise is nine losers, approximately. Therefore, 24 − 3 − 9 comes to twelve tricks, and you can bid 6♠ after checking for keycards first. Cuebidding is not helpful here because South just needs to know he is not missing both the ♠K and the ♣A.

Here is your partner's hand.

$$\spadesuit K J 7 6 2 \quad \heartsuit 6 5 \quad \diamondsuit 8 2 \quad \clubsuit 9 8 7 2$$

With one point for the fifth trump, this is 7 points. Because there is five-card support, a lot of people will rush to 4♠ and to a negative score opposite a minimum opener. However, with the boss suit and not really weak, the responder can try for a positive score. This logic almost always leads to a windfall of matchpoints and here actually gets you to slam.

THE RULE OF 123

So why do I mentally increase the length of my preempt suit with an outside singleton? Well, a hand with a singleton often has one fewer loser. Would I prefer to use a rule that actually counts the losers? Yes, but it all depends on what my partner does.

The losers are calculated as in the LTC section. The rules that count losers are the rule of 123 and the rule of 234. However, these are not as widely used as the length rule. The goal with both of these rules is to ensure that if we are doubled, the opponents will get less than they would score for their game.

At unfavorable vulnerability (hot versus not), they are not vulnerable and you are vulnerable. They can get +420 and down two doubled is too much at 500. Therefore, you preempt expecting to be at most down one. This is the '1' of 123.

Example 2.17 Hot versus Not

♠ K 2   ♡ K Q J 10 9 8 7   ◇ 6 2   ♣ 8 2

In first seat, at unfavorable vulnerability, what do you open?

This hand has six losers. That suggests 3♡ will go down two so pre-empt 2♡ at unfavorable vulnerability. If, like me, you cannot lie about the length in first or second seat (except holding six clubs or a five-card weak two when short in the majors), you must pass and try to come in later. The length rule will let you open 3♡ here, and that might well be right — however, many experts warn against preempting on 7-2-2-2 hands.

At equal vulnerability, both pairs are not vulnerable or both are vulnerable. With both not vulnerable, they can get 420 so down three doubled is too much at 500. Therefore, you can be at most down two. With both vulnerable, they can get 620 and down three doubled is too much at 800. Therefore, you can also be down two. This is the '2' of 123.

Example 2.18 Hot versus Hot or Not versus Not

In first seat, at equal vulnerability, what do you open with this hand?

♠ 7 2   ♡ A J 10 9 8 7 2   ◇ 6 2   ♣ K 2

This has seven losers — 2♡ is down two so open 2♡. I am not saying I agree, but that is what the rule of 123 dictates.

At favorable vulnerability (not versus hot), they are vulnerable and you are not vulnerable. They can get +620 and down four doubled is too much at 800. Therefore, a player preempts to be down three not four. This is the '3' of 123.

Example 2.18 Not versus Hot

In first seat, at favorable vulnerability, what do you open?

♠ 2   ♡ A Q J 10 9 8 7   ◇ 10 9 6 2   ♣ 2

This hand has six losers. The loser count suggests 4♡ is down three, so that is the right call.

THE RULE OF 234

This is the same as the Rule of 123 except it assumes that partner has one trick. If he does not, then the opponents likely have slam if the preempt is a good one with no outside defense. Therefore, the sacrifice, giving up 800, is not so bad. The player bids one level higher than he would with the Rule of 123.

Responses to the Rules of 123 and 234

When partner preempts in first or second seat, and you have values, you are going to think less about keeping the opponents out than getting to your own best spot. First, you need to determine how many losers partner has by looking at the vulnerability and using the particular rule on which the partnership has, *a priori*, decided. Then, count the cover cards — these are the four aces, the four kings and the queen of trumps.

Queens and jacks in side suits are typically useless to a partner who is likely short in these suits. If partner has preempted, he expects to be down a specific number of tricks. You must have sufficient cover cards for partner to make his contract and an additional cover card for every level you are planning to raise.

Example 2.19 Raising a Preempt

The vulnerability is such that partner has bid 3♡ expecting to be down three. How many cover cards (cc) do you have, and what do you bid with the following hands?

a)	♠QJ10	♡J108	◇QJ106	♣QJ10	0cc Pass
b)	♠QJ10	♡KQ10	◇QJ106	♣QJ10	2cc Pass
c)	♠AQ10	♡932	◇A9	♣A5432	3cc Pass
d)	♠A87	♡832	◇AK96	♣KQ10	4cc 4♡
e)	♠7	♡Q42	◇AQ95	♣KQ1098	4cc 4♡
f)	♠7	♡Q42	◇AK95	♣A10982	5cc 4♡
g)	♠—	♡Q542	◇AK95	♣A10982	6cc 6♡

A singleton can be counted as one cover card and a void as two, as long as you have trumps. However, it really comes down to how many ruffs are allowed by the defense, the trumps in dummy and the length partner has in the suit to be ruffed.

You also have to remember that losing trick count is just an estimate assuming good breaks and that half of the finesses work. LTC undervalues prime cards (aces and kings) — Axx and Qxx are both two-loser suits — and does not take into account the degree of fit. So use LTC by all means as one method of hand evaluation, and a guide to the limit of the hand for your side. Just don't treat it as an absolute rule, because it isn't.

Example 2.24 The Length Rule Gets You Too High Sometimes

This hand occurred during a two-session pairs event at the 2015 Denver NABC.

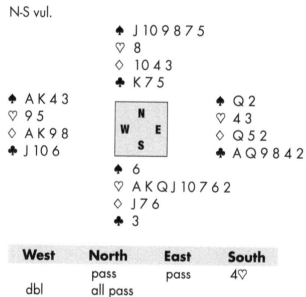

N-S vul.

West	North	East	South
	pass	pass	4♡
dbl	all pass		

East took one look at the vulnerability and passed his partner's takeout double. He remembered the old bridge adage, 'Balanced hands defend'. He could have bid 5♣, but it is not obvious that it is making. Furthermore, 4♡ is down two for +500, which they get whether 5♣ makes or not, and the vulnerability strongly suggested passing. It turned out to be a very good decision because +400 was par for East-West.

Most players make some use of the length rule, but it should be always in the back of your mind that sometimes the rule gets the preemptor too high, as in this example, especially at unfavorable colors. Defending is always a serious alternative to bidding a tenuous game.

Chapter Three

Furthering the Preempt

When a player opens a preempt, his partner first makes an assessment of whether game is possible. If not, the next decision is whether the preempt should be raised — a good guide is the Law of Total Tricks. These direct raises are the only non-forcing bids available. Don't make a direct raise if you are happy doubling the opponents should they come in.

THE LAW OF TOTAL TRICKS (LTT)

I could describe the LTT in depth, but the main result of the Law (this is what most people use, and forget the rest) is that you and your partner can safely contract for the same number of tricks as the total number of cards held in your combined trump suit. When there is an eight-card fit, the partnership should compete to the two-level, and that will either make or be a good sacrifice. With a nine-card fit, the three-level; a ten-card fit, the four-level; an eleven-card fit, the five-level; etc.

The Law supports the idea that the golden fit for competitive bidding and sacrifices is more than eight cards. One caveat, however: Michael Lawrence has written an entire book called *I Fought the Law*. His main objection is that a law should never replace judgment. He also points out that the Law is not close to 100% accurate, and breaks down for many of the same reasons that LTC fails as an absolute guide — fit, prime cards, wasted values, a two-suited fit, etc.

RONF

What is the difference between the following auctions?

West	North	East	South
		3♡	??

West	North	East	South
2♡	pass	3♡	??

South will need the same hand strength to bid in both cases. Therefore, it is incumbent on the partner of the preemptor to raise when possible and make things that much more difficult for the opponents.

RONF stands for 'a raise is the only non-forcing bid' — everything else is forcing. That is the way most people treat auctions after partner has preempted.

West	North	East	South
2♡	pass	3♡	??

West	North	East	South
2♡	pass	4♡	??

West does not know whether East made his 4♡ bid to make or to further impede — but of course, neither do the opponents. It does not matter that West is in the dark, as East is the captain, the player who knows more about both hands than his partner and knows how to place the contract. West's hand is hearts: a preempt is and should be a descriptive bid.

The golden fit for a trump suit is eight cards, but when the bid is made to impede, the golden fit is nine cards or more, and a good guide to follow the Law of Total Tricks.

RAISING A WEAK TWO IN GENERAL

If partner opens a first-seat weak 2♡, and game is out of reach, the number of hearts you have in support determines the level to which you should raise. Two trumps are sufficient for the two-level, three for the three-level, four for the four-level, etc. *Raise right away or not at all.*

Example 3.1 Further Obstruction

At favorable vulnerability partner opens 2♥ with the following hand.

♠ 5 2   ♥ A Q 8 7 5 3   ◊ 9 4 2   ♣ 3 2

West	North	East	South
	2♥	pass	??

What do you bid with each of these hands?

a) ♠ 7 6 4 3 ♥ J 10 9 ◊ 10 8 7 ♣ 9 8 7
b) ♠ 7 ♥ J 10 9 ◊ 10 8 7 ♣ 9 8 7 6 5 4
c) ♠ K Q 4 3 ♥ J 10 9 ◊ A 8 7 ♣ 9 8 7
d) ♠ K Q 3 ♥ J 10 9 6 ◊ A 8 7 6 ♣ 9 8
e) ♠ 3 ♥ J 10 9 6 ◊ 8 7 ♣ 10 9 8 7 6 5
f) ♠ 7 6 4 ♥ J 10 9 6 ◊ 10 8 7 ♣ 9 8 4
g) ♠ A K 10 9 ♥ 6 4 2 ◊ Q J 10 ♣ Q J 10

The Law of Total Tricks is used to determine how far to obstruct the opponents. In cases (a) through (f), the opponents have the outstanding points and heart shortness so obstruction is important. However, pass with (a): there is a risk of being doubled for too much when they may have difficulty in spades. I play bridge as if I am playing good opponents all of the time. In case (f), the flatness and the lack of any high cards suggest that even 3♥ can be doubled for a large telephone number. There are eight losers because there is no entry for a trump finesse. That is 800, which here is not a toll-free number.

In (b), like (e), the good distribution makes up for the sheer weakness of the hand. Raise to 3♥ with (b) and 4♥ with (e).

Hand (c) is a borderline case almost having too much defense, however, the flatness of (c) and (d) is offset by high-card strength. Raise to 3♥ with (c) and 4♥ with (d).

In case (g), it is important not to be in 3♥ down one because if the opponents compete, they may well be going down themselves. This is a poor 13-count, and well short of a hand that can raise to 4♥ with any expectation of making. The minors are poor opposite a preempt on offense, but are likely good on defense when partner rates to be short in these suits. Put it side by side with partner's hand above to see what I mean.

Example 3.2 The Five-level Belongs to the Opponents

E-W vul.

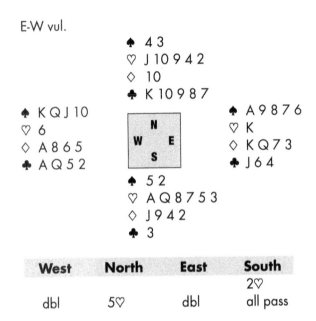

West	North	East	South
			2♡
dbl	5♡	dbl	all pass

How many players sitting East, do you think, will find the double instead of a 5♠ bid? They should, though. First of all, *the five-level belongs to the opponents,* and secondly, East does not have the values needed to underwrite the five-level opposite a minimum double from West. The wasted ♡K is ominous, and in fact here, +300 is the best that can be done once North bids 5♡, since 5♠ goes down one. North's 5♡ bid obeys the Law, and a two-suited hand with five-card support for partner's preempt is exceptional. Some North players (who have not read this book) will not bid the limit of the hand right away — those who only bid 4♡ will probably end up defending 4♠ for a loss of 620.

Example 3.3 The Law is Not Always Right!

N-S vul.

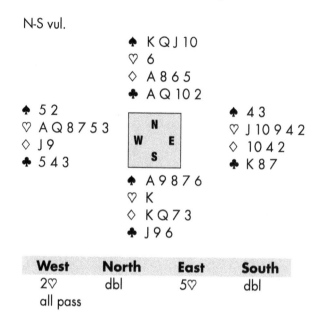

♠ K Q J 10
♥ 6
♦ A 8 6 5
♣ A Q 10 2

♠ 5 2
♥ A Q 8 7 5 3
♦ J 9
♣ 5 4 3

♠ 4 3
♥ J 10 9 4 2
♦ 10 4 2
♣ K 8 7

♠ A 9 8 7 6
♥ K
♦ K Q 7 3
♣ J 9 6

West	North	East	South
2♥	dbl	5♥	dbl
all pass			

The five-level is almost always like a sitting duck. Good players only take the push if they are sure of success. Here, 5♥ doubled is down four for a loss of 800. The Law does not lead to a good result here because, although East's distribution is not the dreaded flat four-triple-three, it is the flattest with a five-card suit. The mirrored shortness is a significant problem.

However, there is a problem because sometimes the Law works with flat hands. Bridge is not played in hindsight, but it turns out that 3♥ by East is a nifty bid, giving his side a chance, although a very slim one, to defend 3♠.

RAISING A THIRD-SEAT WEAK TWO

A third-seat weak two can be five cards long (this was discussed previously). So typically, to raise a third-seat weak two, you should have four cards in support and a singleton somewhere.

Example 3.4 Bid Right Away then Be Silent

Both vul.

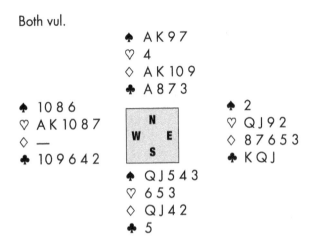

West	North	East	South
		pass	pass
2♥	dbl	4♥	pass
pass	dbl	pass	4♠
all pass			

Too much support in a weak hand is not necessarily good — your side will have little to offer on defense. Here, 5♥ is a good sacrifice (down two), but could well be a silly bid as 6♠ by South is quite likely to make. To set 6♠, West must underlead his top heart honors on the go to get an obvious diamond switch from East. East-West must impede the opponents as much as they deem safe right away, and then they must be quiet. It would be a shame to push them towards a making slam.

IMMEDIACY

Is there anything wrong with the following three auctions?

1.

West	North	East	South
	2♥	pass	pass
2♠	pass	pass	3♥
pass			

When South passed 2♥, had he decided to defend if necessary or did he think West would not compete? He should bid 3♥ right away or not at all.

2.

West	North	East	South
1◇	2♣	2◇	3♣
pass	pass	3◇	4♣

When South bid 3♣, did he already know what he was going to do over 3◇? If he did not, then why not? South should bid 4♣ right away. Some players will step up the auction, as in the bidding shown, in case they can buy the contract at a low level (3♣). This is risky bridge, not knowing whether the opponents can use this space to great advantage. If 3♣ is bid, South should not bid over 3◇. Bidding 4♣ right away works well in the long run.

3.

West	North	East	South
1♡	1♠	1NT	pass
2◇	pass	pass	2♠

In this auction, South delayed a raise because he had a doubleton honor in spades rather than three-card support, but the raise should be made right away or not at all.

West	North	East	South
1♡	1♠	1NT	2♠
??			

Now West needs a much stronger hand to rebid 3◇, and if West passes, East has said his piece and will likely pass 2♠ out.

Summary

In a competitive auction, a player strives to bid the limit of his hand right away to *give the opponents the last guess*. This is a concept Kit Woolsey wrote about in his book, *Matchpoints*. One also tries to hinder opponents' communication so there is uncertainty in their bidding. When a player makes a RONF bid of partner's preempt, he must do it right away or not at all. Therefore, the wrong thing about all three examples is that the bid that South eventually made should have been made right away. When a bid is not ideal, it should not be delayed because then it becomes even worse.

Example 3.5 Stretch to Raise the Preempt

N-S vul.

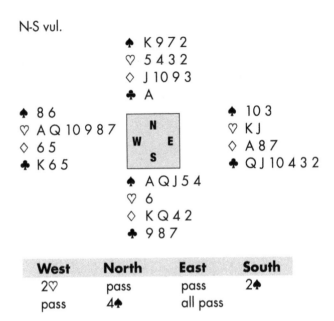

♠ K972
♡ 5432
◇ J1093
♣ A

♠ 86
♡ AQ10987
◇ 65
♣ K65

♠ 103
♡ KJ
◇ A87
♣ QJ10432

♠ AQJ54
♡ 6
◇ KQ42
♣ 987

West	North	East	South
2♡	pass	pass	2♠
pass	4♠	all pass	

Once South balances, North has an easy raise to game. However, does South come in if the bidding goes as follows?

West	North	East	South
2♡	pass	3♡	?

Maybe yes, maybe no. East should not raise without three-card support, as a rule, but if he plans to compete, it is much better to do it right away.

Example 3.6   A Bluff

E-W vul.

```
                    ♠ K 9
                    ♡ A 3 2
                    ◇ A 6 5 4
                    ♣ 9 8 6 3
  ♠ A Q J 2                          ♠ 10 8 7 6 3
  ♡ K Q 10 9        N                ♡ J 8 7 5 4
  ◇ —            W     E             ◇ 3 2
  ♣ K Q 10 7 5       S                ♣ A
                    ♠ 5 4
                    ♡ 6
                    ◇ K Q J 10 9 8 7
                    ♣ J 4 2
```

West	North	East	South
		pass	3◇
dbl	3NT	pass	pass
dbl	pass	4♡	pass
pass	5◇	pass	pass
5♡	pass	pass	6◇
dbl	all pass		

With a big fit for partner's preempt, it's tempting to fool around and try to muddy the waters. Not always the best policy. A bid like 3NT works a lot better when the opponents' points are more evenly split. Here, 3NT did not fool anybody, and in this case, an immediate jump to 5◇ would have been optimum. South's 6◇ was highly undisciplined, and could have been severely punished. If East-West bid their slam, South has to find a spade lead to beat it. So I guess 3NT did fool somebody: South. A preemptor almost always has only one bid to make. The only exception is that a preemptor must bid when his partner makes a forcing call and his RHO passes. However, some like to reraise their own preempt when partner has supported, to prevent the opponents from using Blackwood.

Example 3.7 Another Bluff

In the last example, the 'humorous' 3NT actually has a shot, and in fact makes on a spade lead. This example shows 3NT being bid only on the way to the intended destination.

E-W vul.

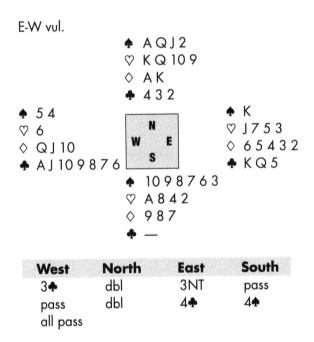

```
                    ♠ A Q J 2
                    ♡ K Q 10 9
                    ◇ A K
                    ♣ 4 3 2
  ♠ 5 4                              ♠ K
  ♡ 6                                ♡ J 7 5 3
  ◇ Q J 10           N              ◇ 6 5 4 3 2
  ♣ A J 10 9 8 7 6  W   E           ♣ K Q 5
                     S
                    ♠ 10 9 8 7 6 3
                    ♡ A 8 4 2
                    ◇ 9 8 7
                    ♣ —
```

West	North	East	South
3♣	dbl	3NT	pass
pass	dbl	4♣	4♠
all pass			

Here, 3NT takes away the same bidding room as 4♣, and East was simply trying to add confusion by a 3NT bid. (Note that even if he believes his partner, West should not double 4♣ — he should bid his own hand not his partner's.) And even if by some miracle East-West can grab a quick nine tricks including seven clubs, that does not mean 4♠ can be defeated.

Chapter Four

Constructive Bidding After a Preempt

PARTNER PREEMPTS

Let's deal first with auctions where partner preempts and you have some cards. When you decide to open a preempt, you should be almost certain that game cannot be made if partner has a minimum opener. Therefore, it makes perfect sense not to try for game with a minimum opener when partner preempts. When game is out of reach, you should consider raising to create further obstruction, as discussed earlier.

When game is a possibility opposite partner's weak two, you may use 2NT as a game try or treat a new suit bid as forcing for one round. Methods such as Ogust and new suit non-forcing are only necessary if preempts are made on garbage suits. This should not apply. When a preempt is made, the suit is usually good, therefore you should play feature-asks and new suit forcing one round. However, for completeness here, Ogust cannot be ignored entirely, as it is popular and you will encounter opponents playing it.

Ogust

This is basic Ogust, but there are many variants:

2♡/2♠	2NT
3♣	Minimum hand, bad suit
3◇	Minimum hand, good suit
3♡	Maximum hand, bad suit
3♠	Maximum hand, good suit
3NT	AKQxxx

A good suit has two of the top three honors, and a bad suit does not. A minimum is 5-7 not vulnerable and 7-8 vulnerable. A maximum is 8-9 not vulnerable and 9-10 vulnerable.

Now that you know Ogust, please forget it. I recommend strongly that you play that over a weak two, 3♣ asks for shortness (singleton or void), and 2NT asks for a feature. You can use either 3NT or 4♣ to show club shortness — I prefer 3NT. A feature is an ace, a king or a queen with a jack. A feature is not shown with a minimum, because a hand with a feature and a minimum has a poor trump suit that should have not been opened as a preempt. Some play that 3NT is bid with a feature, keeping the feature unknown to the opening leader, but it is absolutely necessary to show the suit so partner can determine what values are working together. So is Ogust needed to determine if partner is a minimum or a maximum? No, of course not. Any hand that shows a feature can be assumed to be a maximum. The only time 3NT is the response to the feature request, just like Ogust, is when the suit is AKQxxx. I never have the opportunity to use this bid because I consider a hand with three quick tricks as a one-level opener.

Example 4.1   South Plays 3NT to Avoid a Lead Through

Neither vul.

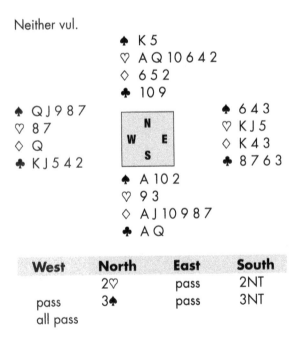

West	North	East	South
	2♡	pass	2NT
pass	3♠	pass	3NT
all pass			

South discovers that partner has a maximum with a spade feature, and decides to play 3NT rather than 4♡ to protect his club holding from a possible opening lead through it. West leads the ♠Q, but now South will not go after hearts, because if East wins, he will attack clubs. Instead, South goes after diamonds to keep East off lead. Eventually, declarer will take two spades, one heart, five diamonds and one club for +400.

Example 4.2   Qxx is Not a Stopper

N-S vul.

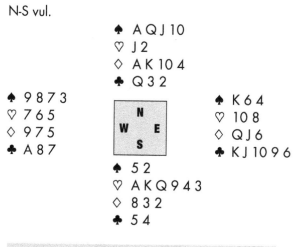

West	North	East	South
		pass	2♡
pass	2NT	pass	3NT
pass	4♡	all pass	

North asked for a feature and South has no feature, but he does have a solid six-card suit. Apparently, not everybody thinks three quick tricks is a one-level opener. I only include the 3NT response to Ogust or the feature-ask out of completeness. Now please forget it. North's ♣Qxx is not a stopper — Q10x is the absolute minimum to count as a stopped suit. Here, East's natural club lead will beat 3NT, but 4♡ makes +620.

Example 4.3 No Short-hand Ruffs

N-S vul.

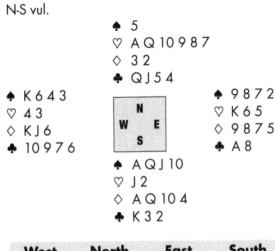

	♠ 5	
	♡ A Q 10 9 8 7	
	◇ 3 2	
	♣ Q J 5 4	
♠ K 6 4 3		♠ 9 8 7 2
♡ 4 3		♡ K 6 5
◇ K J 6		◇ 9 8 7 5
♣ 10 9 7 6		♣ A 8
	♠ A Q J 10	
	♡ J 2	
	◇ A Q 10 4	
	♣ K 3 2	

West	North	East	South
pass	2♡	pass	2NT
pass	3♣	pass	3NT
all pass			

With hearts his shortest suit, South wants to play 3NT unless it means suicide. His 2NT asks for a feature, and when North shows a club feature South tries 3NT. Here declarer will have no trouble coming to nine tricks, and will make more on less than perfect defense.

Example 4.4 Asking for a Feature Was Not Wise

Neither vul.

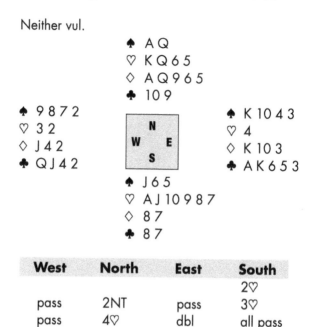

	♠ A Q	
	♡ K Q 6 5	
	◇ A Q 9 6 5	
	♣ 10 9	

♠ 9 8 7 2		♠ K 10 4 3
♡ 3 2		♡ 4
◇ J 4 2		◇ K 10 3
♣ Q J 4 2		♣ A K 6 5 3

	♠ J 6 5
	♡ A J 10 9 8 7
	◇ 8 7
	♣ 8 7

West	North	East	South
			2♡
pass	2NT	pass	3♡
pass	4♡	dbl	all pass

Don't ask for a feature just because you can. North was always bidding 4♡, and should simply have done so. Because South has no feature, East knows his high cards are favorably placed, and can venture a double. If South has the ◇A, East may not get his ◇K.

NEW SUIT FORCING

When a preempt is doubled for takeout and the partner of the preemptor is short, there are two short hands. A takeout double shows shortness and therefore the other opponent is long and may convert the double to penalty. However, the partner of the preemptor cannot save partner since partner chose to preempt (more on this later). Therefore, even if RHO makes a call, a new suit is forcing one round.

Example 4.5   Educated Guesswork

N-S vul.

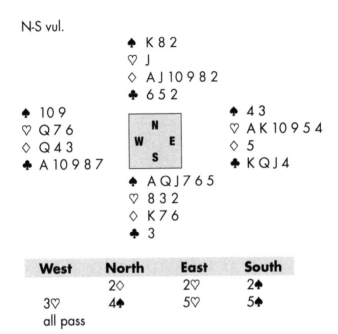

West	North	East	South
	2◊	2♡	2♠
3♡	4♠	5♡	5♠
all pass			

It looks like a battle of the round suits versus the pointed suits. South's 2♠ bid is forcing one round; once West bids, North could pass, but not with that hand. On this layout 4♡ is cold and so is 5♠. And over 5♠, 6♡ is a very satisfactory sacrifice, but I would be wary of pushing North-South to 6♠. It is unlikely there is a heart void, because a North who knows what he is doing would not preempt with a void or a four-card major, but why chance it? The best move is to let 5♠ play and see if it can be set.

Yes, in one breath, I say that 6♠ may make, and in another, I say that perhaps 5♠ can be set. That is very indicative of the uncertainty of high-level bidding. Sometimes, it involves guesswork, but I suggest that you make it educated guesswork.

Example 4.6 The Preemptor Should Not Raise with a Doubleton

N-S vul.

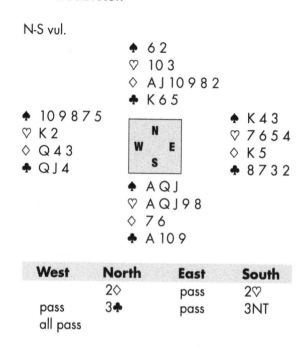

```
              ♠ 6 2
              ♡ 10 3
              ◇ A J 10 9 8 2
              ♣ K 6 5
♠ 10 9 8 7 5              ♠ K 4 3
♡ K 2              N        ♡ 7 6 5 4
◇ Q 4 3       W       E     ◇ K 5
♣ Q J 4           S        ♣ 8 7 3 2
              ♠ A Q J
              ♡ A Q J 9 8
              ◇ 7 6
              ♣ A 10 9
```

West	North	East	South
	2◇	pass	2♡
pass	3♣	pass	3NT
all pass			

South is asking North for three-card heart support. North need not rush to show two-card support. Without three hearts, North has two options: he either bids a feature with a maximum, or returns to 3◇ with a minimum. If he holds three hearts, North also has two options: 3♡ with a minimum and 4♡ with a maximum. The reader must note that I did not say four hearts because *first or second-seat preempts do not include a four-card major*. Period. Here they reach 3NT, and declarer loses a diamond and a heart for +660.

Example 4.7   Help Partner Find the Best Suit

E-W vul.

```
              ♠ A K J 10 9 8
              ♡ K 4 3
              ◇ A 2
              ♣ A 6
♠ 7                              ♠ Q 4 3 2
♡ 7 5 2          N              ♡ 6
◇ Q 10 5 4 3   W   E            ◇ K J 9 8
♣ Q J 5 4        S              ♣ K 8 7 3
              ♠ 6 5
              ♡ A Q J 10 9 8
              ◇ 7 6
              ♣ 10 9 2
```

West	North	East	South
			2♡
pass	2♠	pass	3♡
pass	4NT	pass	5♣
pass	5◇	pass	5NT
pass	6♡	all pass	

Here it is critical that spades are not raised on two-card support because 2♠ does not deny heart support. South denies three spades so North's side suit can probably be set up for five tricks via ruffing. RKCB tells North about the ♡AQ, but he cannot be sure that 7♡ is a good spot — yes, South could have the ♠Q, but a singleton small spade would not be a good holding. It would be a shame to go down in a grand because a ruffing finesse loses when bidding a small slam is close to a top.

Don't bid grand slams on guesses. Bid them only when thirteen tricks can be counted. Here the layout is friendly, and declarer will get five spades, six hearts and two minor-suit aces for thirteen tricks. Note that if South raises spades, 6♠ will be down one if a minor is led.

THE RULE OF SEVENTEEN

Numerical rules are no substitute for judgment, but the Rule of 17 is a rough guide to start you thinking. When partner opens a weak two, he can be raised to the four-level (game in a major) when your trump holding plus your HCP total 17 or more. Like many such, the rule has a tendency to fail when the points are quacky. When partner preempts, the cover cards are important. Queens and jacks in side suits are often useless opposite a hand that preempts.

Example 4.8   Too Many First and Second Round Losers

E-W vul.

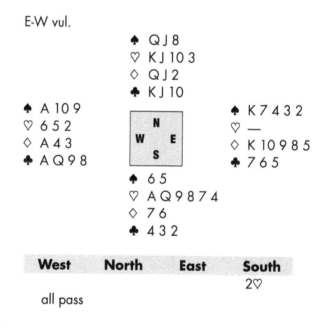

West	North	East	South
			2♡

all pass

North has 14 HCP and four trumps, so according to the rule, he should bid 4♡. However, North must recognize his points are quacky and his distribution is four-triple-three. South has a very typical weak two, and 4♡ has no play — something North could envisage just by imagining South's hand. North will, however, be happy to double if the opponents step into the auction. Queens and jacks in side suits are very useful on defense, especially when partner is likely short in those suits.

Example 4.9   Just Bid Game

N-S vul.

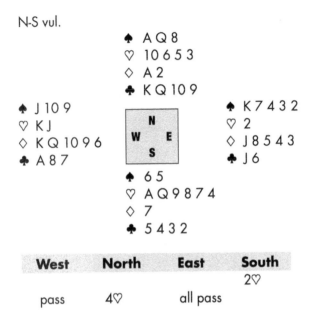

West	North	East	South
			2♡
pass	4♡	all pass	

With four trumps and 15 HCP, the rule says North should bid game, and this time it is right. There's no need to go through any kind of 2NT sequence which might give the opponents a chance to make a lead-directing double, or find a good save.

COVER CARDS

The methods discussed so far essentially apply only to weak twos. For higher preempts, cover cards are considered for raises to game. This was discussed earlier in the section on the rules of 123 and 234. The cover cards are, as before: the aces, the kings and the trump queen. A singleton is one cover card, and a void is two cover cards assuming sufficient trumps are held. In general, the partner of the preemptor needs three cover cards not vulnerable and two cover cards vulnerable to let opener make the preempt, and one more for each level raised.

Example 4.10 A Vulnerable Preempt

N-S vul.

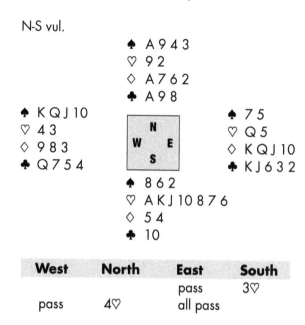

| ♠ A 9 4 3 |
| ♡ 9 2 |
| ◇ A 7 6 2 |
| ♣ A 9 8 |

♠ K Q J 10   ♠ 7 5
♡ 4 3   ♡ Q 5
◇ 9 8 3   ◇ K Q J 10
♣ Q 7 5 4   ♣ K J 6 3 2

| ♠ 8 6 2 |
| ♡ A K J 10 8 7 6 |
| ◇ 5 4 |
| ♣ 10 |

West	North	East	South
		pass	3♡
pass	4♡	all pass	

North has three cover cards and can raise partner to game. Vulnerable preempts usually need only two cover cards to make, and North has three.

Example 4.11 You Thought About 3NT — Really?

E-W vul.

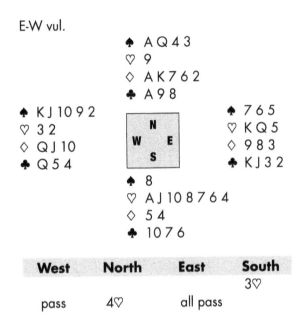

	♠ A Q 4 3	
	♡ 9	
	◇ A K 7 6 2	
	♣ A 9 8	

♠ K J 10 9 2   ♠ 7 6 5
♡ 3 2   ♡ K Q 5
◇ Q J 10   ◇ 9 8 3
♣ Q 5 4   ♣ K J 3 2

♠ 8
♡ A J 10 8 7 6 4
◇ 5 4
♣ 10 7 6

West	North	East	South
			3♡
pass	4♡	all pass	

I can hardly recommend making a one-card raise of partner's preempt a regular practice, but 3NT would be a ridiculous bid. The heart suit will not be solid, and South is unlikely to have side cards that can serve as entries, so his hand will provide essentially no tricks as dummy. A notrump game is only a reasonable bid if North can see where nine tricks can be made in his own hand. North has four cover cards to cover six of South's side-suit cards. If partner can keep the trump suit to one loser or reduce the side suit losers to one with two trump losers, 4♡ will make. Here the hearts are friendly, and declarer can get home even on a club lead.

Example 4.12 A Singleton is a Cover Card

Neither vul.

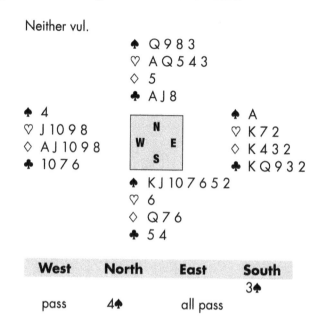

West	North	East	South
			3♠
pass	4♠	all pass	

North has four cover cards (♠Q, ♡A, ◊5, ♣A) and can bid game. Declarer loses a diamond, a club and a spade for +420.

Example 4.13 An Easy Raise to Game

Neither vul.

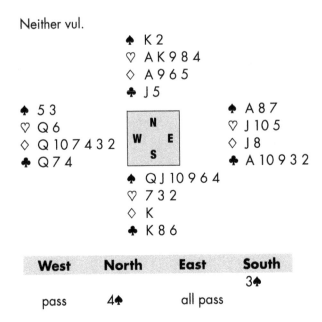

♠ K 2
♡ A K 9 8 4
♢ A 9 6 5
♣ J 5

♠ 5 3
♡ Q 6
♢ Q 10 7 4 3 2
♣ Q 7 4

♠ A 8 7
♡ J 10 5
♢ J 8
♣ A 10 9 3 2

♠ Q J 10 9 6 4
♡ 7 3 2
♢ K
♣ K 8 6

West	North	East	South
			3♠
pass	4♠	all pass	

This hand came up in an ACBL matchpoint speedball tourney on BBO. Even if partner opened 2♠, North would bid 4♠ according to the Rule of 17, and 3♠ shows an extra trick over 2♠. In this case, four cover cards gave him an easy raise to 4♠.

PREEMPTING A PREEMPT

A pretty simple rule of thumb is that *you do not preempt a preempt*. Non-raise action over partner's preempt typically shows strength, not another preempt in a different suit. However, I would not always assume players do the right thing.

Example 4.14 When and How to Run

N-S vul.

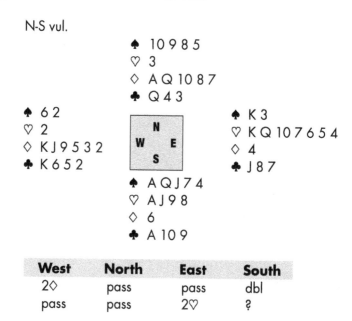

	♠ 10 9 8 5	
	♡ 3	
	◊ A Q 10 8 7	
	♣ Q 4 3	
♠ 6 2		♠ K 3
♡ 2		♡ K Q 10 7 6 5 4
◊ K J 9 5 3 2		◊ 4
♣ K 6 5 2		♣ J 8 7
	♠ A Q J 7 4	
	♡ A J 9 8	
	◊ 6	
	♣ A 10 9	

West	North	East	South
2◊	pass	pass	dbl
pass	pass	2♡	?

What do you do when you plan to open 3♡ but partner makes a 2◊ preempt ahead of you? Look at the layout above. First of all, holding a stiff diamond, 2◊ should warn you to stay out of this auction. Secondly, bidding hearts directly shows a good forward-going hand, which East does not have. So 2♡ can be bid only after 2◊ is doubled for penalty. No, a player does not rescue partner as a general rule, but a good seven-card suit is an exception. There is another must: West must not go back to diamonds because of heart shortness. Flip-flopping is for logic circuits, not bridge. I am pretty sure East does not want to play 3◊ doubled.

Here, 2◊ rates to go for 800 and 2♡ only 500. You might think that even 800 is a good sacrifice, since twelve tricks are available in spades. However, even if North does not convert the takeout double to penalty (by passing), it's highly unlikely North-South are going to bid slam. If they do, they'll feel themselves very lucky to have made it.

Example 4.15 McCabe for the Lead

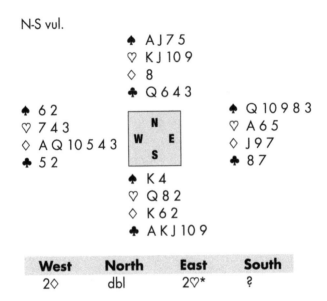

N-S vul.

	♠ A J 7 5	
	♡ K J 10 9	
	◇ 8	
	♣ Q 6 4 3	
♠ 6 2		♠ Q 10 9 8 3
♡ 7 4 3		♡ A 6 5
◇ A Q 10 5 4 3		◇ J 9 7
♣ 5 2		♣ 8 7
	♠ K 4	
	♡ Q 8 2	
	◇ K 6 2	
	♣ A K J 10 9	

West	North	East	South
2◇	dbl	2♡*	?

The methods I have recommended above (2NT for a feature, new suit forcing one round) are not the only possibilities over partner's weak two. The McCabe Adjunct is a popular gadget when partner's weak two is doubled for takeout. In this method, new suits show a raise to the indicated level, and are lead-directing. Here, East is willing to play 3◇ and bids 2♡ as a lead-direct so diamonds can be led through South, the potential 3NT bidder. Now South would be ill-advised to gamble on notrump, and North-South will do well to find their 5♣ game.

Example 4.16 McCabe Saves the Day

N-S vul.

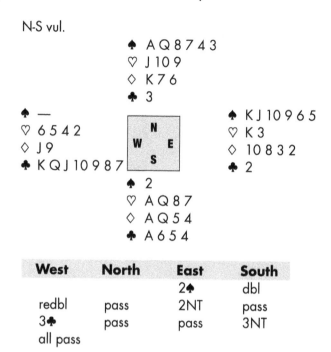

	♠ AQ8743
	♡ J109
	◇ K76
	♣ 3

♠ —   ♠ KJ10965
♡ 6542   ♡ K3
◇ J9   ◇ 10832
♣ KQJ10987   ♣ 2

	♠ 2
	♡ AQ87
	◇ AQ54
	♣ A654

West	North	East	South
		2♠	dbl
redbl	pass	2NT	pass
3♣	pass	pass	3NT
all pass			

The best part of McCabe is the redouble, which asks partner to bid the next step up — usually the start of a one-suited runout. West corrects here to 3♣, which is down only three for -500, a nice sacrifice because 3NT makes ten tricks for +630. South knows spades are stopped because partner was willing to play 2♠ redoubled, but it will take some nerve to bid 3NT now opposite a partner who has shown nothing but length in spades.

RHO Preempts

To double in the direct seat over a weak two, a player needs a good 14 HCP and the correct shape. To take action in the direct seat over a weak three, a player needs a good 17 HCP and the correct shape. These numbers for bidding over any preempt are just a guide, and it is the playing strength, a little harder to count, that is the most important factor.

The best shape is a singleton or void in the preempt suit and four cards in each of the unbid suits. A good shape is two or fewer in the doubled suit and three or four cards in any unbid suit. The less ideal the shape, the more high-card points are needed. Points in the preempt suit are not good points. A double or overcall shows the same strength, just a different shape: overcaller should have a good five- or six-card suit, depending on the level.

Example 4.17 Bidding Directly over a Weak Two

RHO, in first seat, opens 2♡, neither vulnerable. What do you bid with each of the following hands?

a) ♠ A K 10 9 8 ♡ 9 ◇ A 10 5 ♣ K 10 6 5
b) ♠ A K 10 9 ♡ 2 ◇ A 10 5 3 ♣ K 10 6 5
c) ♠ A K 10 ♡ 9 2 ◇ A 10 5 3 ♣ Q 10 6 5
d) ♠ J 9 3 2 ♡ 2 ◇ K J 5 3 ♣ A Q J 5
e) ♠ J 10 9 8 ♡ 2 ◇ A 10 5 3 ♣ A 10 5 2
f) ♠ Q J 10 9 ♡ 2 ◇ A 10 5 3 ♣ A K 10 5
g) ♠ A Q J 9 ♡ Q J ◇ J 5 2 ♣ Q 8 6 5
h) ♠ A Q 2 ♡ Q 2 ◇ Q J 5 2 ♣ Q J 6 5
i) ♠ Q 7 6 5 4 ♡ A K ◇ J 5 ♣ K 10 6 3
j) ♠ Q 10 9 5 ♡ A K ◇ K 10 5 ♣ K 10 6 3
k) ♠ Q 10 9 5 ♡ A K ◇ 10 5 ♣ A K J 10 6
l) ♠ Q 10 9 5 ♡ 9 2 ◇ A K J 10 6 ♣ A K

In (a), action is obvious with heart shortness and good controls (a singleton, aces and kings). Overcalling 2♠ is reasonable, but a double gives partner more options when he has spade shortness.

If only all of your doubles had the shape like the one in (b), (d) and (f). Holding four cards in every unbid suit is ideal but three cards is okay, as in (c), where again I would double. Hand (l) is an interesting case because the four spades suggest a double, and if partner bids 3♣ you are strong enough to bid 3◇ over it. However, most of the time when you double, the unbid suits should be three or four cards long. Hand (e) has the ideal shape for a double, but is really on the weak side even though the two aces are nice; I would pass.

Honors in the opponent's suit may lead to a pass especially if the honors are wasted like in (g) and (h). Bidding notrump becomes an option in (j) and (k) because the honors in the opponent's suit are double stoppers and you have the required strength: bid 2NT on (j) and 3NT on (k). Honors in the opponent's suit are double-edged swords. They may prevent the opponent making their contract, but may not be much use on offense, except in notrump of course.

With hand (i), you are under strength for 2NT and a diamond response to a double cannot be tolerated. You might be prepared to overcall 2♠, but on a suit that bad I would not. Take your medicine and pass.

Example 4.18 Bidding Directly over a Weak Three

RHO, in first seat, opens 3♡, neither vulnerable. What do you bid with each the following hands?

a)   ♠ A J 10 9 8   ♡ 9   ◇ A 10 5   ♣ K 10 6 5
b)   ♠ A K 10 9 8 7   ♡ 2   ◇ A 10 5   ♣ K 10 9
c)   ♠ A K 10   ♡ K 2   ◇ A 10 5 3   ♣ Q 10 6 5
d)   ♠ A J   ♡ K 3   ◇ A 3   ♣ A K Q 10 9 6 5
e)   ♠ Q 10 9 8   ♡ 2   ◇ A 10 5 3   ♣ A K 10 5
f)   ♠ A K 10 9   ♡ Q J   ◇ Q 10 5   ♣ K 10 6 5
g)   ♠ A Q 10   ♡ Q J   ◇ K Q 10 2   ♣ A K 10 5
h)   ♠ Q 7 6 5 4   ♡ A K   ◇ A K   ♣ J 10 6 3
i)   ♠ Q 10 9 5   ♡ A K   ◇ K 10 5   ♣ K 10 6 3
j)   ♠ Q 10 9 5   ♡ A K   ◇ A 5   ♣ A K J 10 6
k)   ♠ Q 10 9 5   ♡ 9 2   ◇ A K J 10 6   ♣ A K
l)   ♠ A K Q 10 9 8 7   ♡ 2   ◇ A 10   ♣ K Q 10

In (a), some may be tempted to bid 3♠, but a double gives partner some flexibility because there is support for three suits, and partner may choose to convert the double to penalty by passing. When my partner doubles hearts, I am never afraid to bid a three-card spade suit.

An overcall and a double are similar strengths, just different shapes. A double followed by a bid is stronger. Hand (b) is a 3♠ overcall, a good six-card suit. Doubles tend to be less appropriate when the unbid suits differ significantly in length (usually by two or more).

Double with (c). Even though adverse honors are bad, the ♡K is well-positioned and is likely a trick, although I would prefer it in another suit. Doubles are best when there are two cards or fewer in the doubled suit and three or four cards in each unbid suit.

In (d), there are ten tricks in 3NT on a heart lead. It is best to be able to count nine tricks when you make this bid over a preempt, especially when there is only one stopper.

Hand (e) is getting close to being too weak to bid, but it has ideal shape and good controls, so double.

In (f), wasted honors in the opponent's suit are an anathema and strongly indicate a pass. In (g), the outside strength makes up for the wasted heart honors, and I would double.

If the honors are moved from the heart suit, hand (h) certainly warrants action. As it is, you are really too strong to pass, but nothing really appeals: 3♠, double and 3NT all have their drawbacks. They say you can't be perfect over preempts, and this is a good case. Roll the dice, pick one, and hope it works out.

Hand (i) is a borderline case. The added club control and spade intermediates compared to (h) make it a fairly clear double.

With hands (j) and (k), start with a double. Over a spade response, a cuebid, showing support and strength, is the rebid. With (j), you may be tempted to bid 3NT over partner's 4◇, but even if this were legal, 3NT is unlikely to have much play — better to pass and hope for the best. With (k), you can bid 4◇ over 4♣, with some hope of a plus score. If your clubs and diamonds are reversed, it becomes a very strong pass. Preempts work, after all.

On hand (l), just bid 4♠. It is that much stronger than (b).

Example 4.19 Gotcha!

N-S vul.

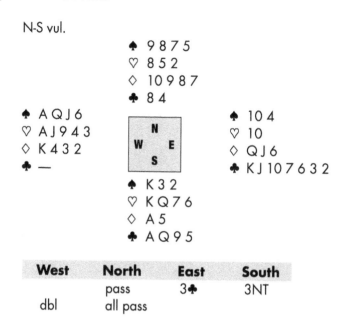

	♠ 9 8 7 5		
	♡ 8 5 2		
	◊ 10 9 8 7		
	♣ 8 4		

♠ A Q J 6   ♠ 10 4
♡ A J 9 4 3   ♡ 10
◊ K 4 3 2   ◊ Q J 6
♣ —   ♣ K J 10 7 6 3 2

♠ K 3 2
♡ K Q 7 6
◊ A 5
♣ A Q 9 5

West	North	East	South
	pass	3♣	3NT
dbl	all pass		

Preempts cause problems, and you won't always solve them correctly. Here, South chose the wrong course of action, but on another day he might have been quite right. It turned out that passing 3♣ would have been the best choice. If you are going to choose to pass with a hand like South's, then partner must balance aggressively if he is short in clubs. For example, North should double in the balancing seat with the following hand:

♠ A 10 9 6   ♡ J 10 4 3   ◊ K Q 3 2   ♣ 3

Example 4.20 Double and Bid Your Suit Over the Preempt

Both vul.

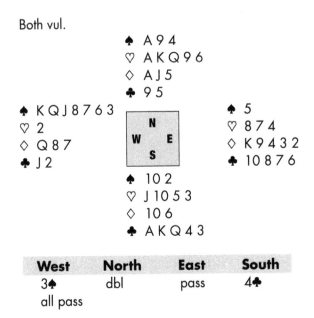

	♠ A 9 4		
	♡ A K Q 9 6		
	◇ A J 5		
	♣ 9 5		

♠ K Q J 8 7 6 3   ♠ 5
♡ 2   ♡ 8 7 4
◇ Q 8 7   ◇ K 9 4 3 2
♣ J 2   ♣ 10 8 7 6

♠ 10 2
♡ J 10 5 3
◇ 10 6
♣ A K Q 4 3

West	North	East	South
3♠	dbl	pass	4♣
all pass			

This deal came up during a local team game. At one table, North doubled, and South bid 4♣, which was passed out and made an overtrick.

At the other table, North overcalled 4♡. While that won 11 IMPs, the auction was correct at neither table.

North has almost the right strength for a 4♡ overcall, but because his hand is all prime cards (four keycards and the queen of trumps,) he should start with a double. Then the bidding might go as follows:

West	North	East	South
3♠	dbl	pass	4♡
pass	4♠	pass	5♣
pass	6♡	all pass	

In response to any takeout double, South must bid a four-card major before a five-card minor. There is one thing about preempts: they make a player hone his bidding.

Example 4.21 Two-level Four-card Overcall

N-S vul.

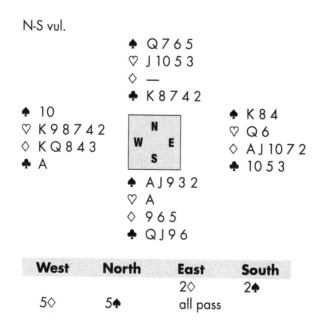

	♠ Q765	
	♡ J1053	
	◇ —	
	♣ K8742	

♠ 10		♠ K84
♡ K98742		♡ Q6
◇ KQ843		◇ AJ1072
♣ A		♣ 1053

	♠ AJ932	
	♡ A	
	◇ 965	
	♣ QJ96	

West	North	East	South
		2◇	2♠
5◇	5♠	all pass	

This deal demonstrates the difficulty of bidding over even such a mild pre-empt as a weak two in diamonds. If his side is going to get into the auction, South has to make an unorthodox overcall with a very poor suit — one that most would not venture except at matchpoints, or maybe in need of a swing at teams.

The majority action here would be a pass. The double, which gives partner more options, is not even considered here because an unbid major contains fewer than three cards.

Because of South's heart shortness, 2♠ makes it harder for West or North to venture a heart call. North will likely stay out of the auction with spade shortness. However, he has good spade support and superb distribution to make a 5♠ call.

Yes, preempts work. Although 5♠ makes, any time the opponents have to make difficult choices, a preempt has worked. if South's hand had been the following (which is 3 HCP stronger) he certainly would have passed 2◇:

♠ AQJ2 ♡ AJ ◇ 965 ♣ QJ96

LHO Preempts

To take action in the balancing seat over a weak two, a player needs a good 10 HCP and the correct shape. To take action in the balancing seat over a weak three, a player needs a good 13 HCP and the correct shape. As mentioned above, the best shape is a singleton or void in the preemptive suit and four cards in each unbid suit. Less ideal, but still correct, is two or fewer in the doubled suit and three or four cards in all unbid suits. The less ideal the shape, the more high-card points are needed.

Example 4.22 Balancing over a Weak Two

Both vul.

West	North	East	South
2♡	pass	pass	??

What should South bid with each of the following hands?

a) ♠ A K 10 9 8 7 ♡ 9 ◇ 10 5 ♣ K 10 6 5
b) ♠ 10 9 5 4 3 2 ♡ K 2 ◇ A K ♣ 10 6 5
c) ♠ A K 10 9 8 ♡ 9 3 2 ◇ A 10 5 3 ♣ 5
d) ♠ J 9 5 3 2 ♡ 4 3 ◇ A K ♣ A 6 5 2
e) ♠ Q 10 9 8 ♡ A Q ◇ A 10 5 3 ♣ K 10 5
f) ♠ A K 10 9 ♡ 3 2 ◇ 10 9 5 ♣ K 10 6 5
g) ♠ A J 10 ♡ Q 2 ◇ K 10 5 2 ♣ K 10 6 5
h) ♠ 9 5 4 ♡ A K 3 ◇ 10 5 2 ♣ K 10 6 3
i) ♠ 9 5 4 ♡ A K 3 ◇ A 5 2 ♣ K 10 6 3
j) ♠ K 9 5 4 ♡ A K 3 ◇ A 5 2 ♣ 10 6 2
k) ♠ K 9 5 4 ♡ 3 ◇ A 7 6 5 2 ♣ 10 6 2
l) ♠ K 9 5 4 ♡ 4 3 2 ◇ A 7 6 5 ♣ 3 2
m) ♠ A K Q 10 9 4 3 ♡ 2 ◇ A K 10 ♣ 6 5

With hand (a), bid 2♠. This hand is much lighter than a direct overcall, but it has the correct shape and partner could be passing with a good hand but the wrong shape to come in.

With hands (b) and (d) you should pass. The strength is in the short suits and the long suit is very poor. If the opponents win the contract, partner could give up a trick if he has a spade honor and leads the suit.

In (c), it is slightly dangerous to come in holding three hearts, but nothing is without risk. Nevertheless, you have a good spade suit with good intermediates and have to protect partner by bidding 2♠.

With hand (e), you could double, but 2NT is a better description. It's also good to have two stoppers (although Axx works in a pinch, as two hold-ups may break communication between the player with entries and the preemptor).

Hand (f) is getting light in points, so some may pass, but it is a double as long as partner realizes a balancing double is lighter than a direct double. Partner must not hang you for being competitive with a reasonable shape.

Wasted honors in the opponent's suit are a detriment and are not counted in (g), but you still have enough to double. Strength in the preemptive suit that is not wasted may be less of a detriment, but that strength is not optimally placed in hands (h) to (j). The poor three-card spade suit is another flaw and a large reason to pass in (h) and (i). Although (j) is a marginal double, four cards in spades tip the balance in favor for me.

While hand (k) is the correct shape, it is light on points and I would pass. Hand (l) is not only light but has bad shape with three cards in the opponent's suit, so pass is clear.

With (m), jump to 4♠, which shows a stronger hand than the lower overcalls. It is also promises a self-sufficient suit or nearly so. With the same strength but a weaker suit, you can double and then bid your suit, which is stronger than bidding the suit directly.

Example 4.23 Balancing over a Weak Three

Both vul.

West	North	East	South
3♡	pass	pass	??

What should South bid with each of the following hands?

a) ♠A K 10 9 8   ♡9   ◇A 10 5   ♣K 10 6 5
b) ♠A K 10 9   ♡4   ◇A 10 5 3   ♣J 10 6 5
c) ♠A K 10   ♡9 3 2   ◇A 10   ♣Q 10 6 5 2
d) ♠J 9 3 2   ♡2   ◇A 10 5 3   ♣A 9 6 5
e) ♠Q 10 9   ♡3 2   ◇A K 10 3   ♣A 10 5 2
f) ♠A K Q 10 9 4 3   ♡2   ◇A K 10   ♣6 5
g) ♠A J 10   ♡Q 2   ◇K 10 5 2   ♣K 10 6 5
h) ♠Q 10 9 5 4   ♡A K   ◇10 5   ♣K 10 6 3
i) ♠10 9 3   ♡Q 2   ◇A K 10 3   ♣A 10 5 2
j) ♠Q 10 9 5   ♡A K   ◇10 5   ♣A J 10 6 2
k) ♠Q 10 9 5   ♡9 2   ◇A K J 10 6   ♣A K

If only you always held a hand like (a) in this auction. It has good controls, including heart shortness, and good intermediates. Furthermore, in a crunch, only one dummy entry will be needed (to lead up to the ♣K). Bidding 3♠ is marginally better than doubling because you strongly prefer to play in spades over diamonds — if you double, partner may bid a four-card diamond suit even if he has three spades.

With (b), a double is ideal because you have four cards in all the unbid suits. Bridge would be easy if all the hands were like this one.

In (c), the first flaw is a doubleton in an unbid suit. The second flaw, only three spades not four, warrants a pass.

Hand (d) is very light on high cards, and has to pass. Hand (e) is strong enough, and has acceptable shape for a double.

Hand (f) is loaded with high cards and a self-sufficient seven-card suit. It needs very little (the ◇Q, the ♣K or either missing ace, for example) to make game. Therefore, 4♠ is the bid.

Hand (g), like (i), is a pass because it has a wasted heart honor, and the spade suit is only three cards long.

Hand (h) is a difficult one. It clearly has the strength to do something, but the shape and the possession of 7 HCP in the opponent's suit make a bid difficult. A double cannot stand a diamond response and the spade suit is poor; however, I hold my nose and bid 3♠.

Hand (j) has too much strength in the opponent's suit, along with a doubleton diamond. The ♡AK are not wasted, but they would be better placed in one of the long suits. I would pass.

On hand (k), you should double and then take another bid. It is important to make sure the bidding distinguishes between hands like (b), (f) and (k). So here, 4◊ will be the rebid if partner responds 4♣, while a spade response will be raised to game.

JUMPS OVER A PREEMPT

A simple jump over a preempt is not a weak bid. It is a stronger bid than an overcall by at least an ace. When preempts are involved, there is not always enough room to double and then bid your suit to show a very strong hand. A jump requires an ace more than an overcall while a double jump would require a couple of aces more. Later in this book we'll discuss a conventional use for a jump over a preempt: Leaping Michaels.

Example 4.24 'Is that Preemptive?' the Opponent Asked

This is a good example from an ACBL IMP speedball tourney on BBO.

N-S vul.

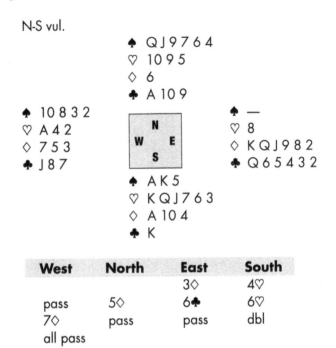

```
              ♠ Q J 9 7 6 4
              ♡ 10 9 5
              ♢ 6
              ♣ A 10 9
♠ 10 8 3 2                        ♠ —
♡ A 4 2          N               ♡ 8
♢ 7 5 3       W     E            ♢ K Q J 9 8 2
♣ J 8 7          S               ♣ Q 6 5 4 3 2
              ♠ A K 5
              ♡ K Q J 7 6 3
              ♢ A 10 4
              ♣ K
```

West	North	East	South
		3♢	4♡
pass	5♢	6♣	6♡
7♢	pass	pass	dbl
all pass			

No, South is not preempting a preempt. With a preempt of his own, he must pass and come in later if practical. Jumping over a preempt shows a stronger hand than just bidding 3♡. The 5♢ cuebid is interesting. The reason 5♣ is skipped is that partner is likely looking at two or three diamonds and a club cuebid will tell him nothing about the likely problem diamond suit. It is certainly not normal to bypass a suit where you have a control, but there is not a lot of room, and partner should understand this.

East has quite a powerful distributional hand. He could open 3♣ as in 2.10, but that tactic works better in third seat, and here a diamond lead is clearly preferable to a club lead. He introduces clubs at his second turn, and West, with a double fit, decides on a 7Dx sacrifice. This is down three for -500. Meanwhile, 6♡ is down one on a spade lead, but West will have to find that without a Lightner double, as they may run to a cold spade slam! Even so, the seven-level sacrifice for -500 beats -650.

Example 4.25 Michaels, Like a Jump, is a Show of Strength

Neither vul.

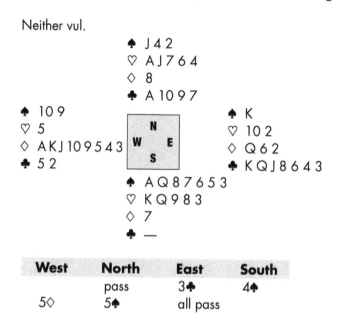

♠ J 4 2
♥ A J 7 6 4
♦ 8
♣ A 10 9 7

♠ 10 9
♥ 5
♦ A K J 10 9 5 4 3
♣ 5 2

♠ K
♥ 10 2
♦ Q 6 2
♣ K Q J 8 6 4 3

♠ A Q 8 7 6 5 3
♥ K Q 9 8 3
♦ 7
♣ —

West	North	East	South
	pass	3♣	4♠
5◊	5♠	all pass	

This hand occurred during the top KO bracket of a Victoria regional tournament. East-West lost 480 for 5♠+1, and their teammates got +980 for 6♡ making. They gained +11 IMPs. South, not in slam, made a mistake in the bidding — he should have bid 4♣ showing both majors, and then the auction could have gone as follows.

West	North	East	South
	pass	3♣	4♣
5◊	6♡	??	

Since 7◊ doubled is down 800, East-West can save 3 IMPs by taking the save, but the damage has been done. Once North knows about his partner's length in both majors, his hand becomes enormous.

Example 4.26 Did the Opponent Think 4♡ Was a Preempt?

Neither vul.

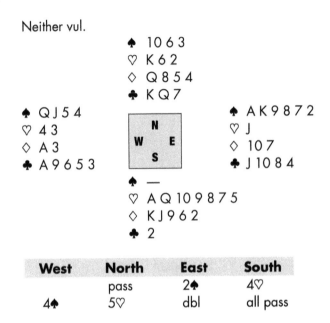

	North	East	South
West	pass	2♠	4♡
4♠	5♡	dbl	all pass

This deal was played during an ACBL IMP speedball tourney on BBO. East has a preempt most players will make. His hand is all in spades with no side defense and very short in the unbid major. The two-suited nature of his hand will make the hand more playable on offense. It actually is too strong for a preempt because it offers a good play for game opposite 10 HCP from partner.

South has a powerful offensive hand as well, certainly one that is stronger than its 10 HCP imply. Opposite a couple of the right cards from partner it could make a slam. East should not double, because he has already bid his entire hand, and his partner is better positioned to make the 'defend or bid on' decision.

If he passes, his partner may find a successful sacrifice in 5♠ for a loss of 300. Meanwhile, 5♡ doubled makes for 650 instead of 450. This example shows that high-card points are not in themselves indicative of the potential of the hands. Both sides have a two-suited fit, and values are mostly not wasted, except for clubs. It is very important therefore that East-West do not allow South to play hearts at the four- or five-level.

Example 4.27 A Pass is Required

So what do you do if you have a preempt and your RHO preempts? You must pass, because a simple overcall shows strength and a jump overcall shows more strength. "How can I make the deal harder for my partner?" should be farthest from your mind.

E-W vul.

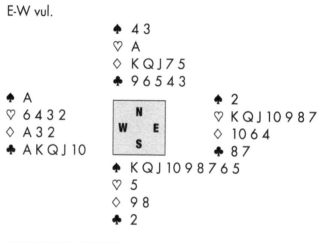

West	North	East	South
		3♡	pass
4♡	pass	pass	4♠
5♡	5♠	pass	pass
dbl	all pass		

With North still to bid, South must not muddy the waters in case his partner has high cards. If North is a passed hand, South can do what he likes. Even 5♠ is not out of the question, but it risks West bidding 6♡, and then South had better find a diamond lead! West's 4♡ could actually be a colossal underbid. If East has ♡AKJ10987, 7NT is cold. Perhaps West is the victim of East's preempt, but 4♣ as Keycard (over all but club preempts) solves the problem. With the bidding shown, West takes the sure plus by doubling 5♠.

DOUBLES AROUND PREEMPTS

Doubles of preempts are generally takeout up to a certain level. I like to play takeout, negative and responsive doubles to 4♡ inclusive, while 4NT over 4♠ is takeout with equal-level correction.

However, when an opponent has bid over our preempt, doubles are penalty. The preemptor can even double for penalty based on partner's bidding and his holding in the doubled suit, but that is rare. Doubles of opponent's overcall cannot be asking for a second suit, as good preempts usually do not have one.

Example 4.28 Gotcha Again!

E-W vul.

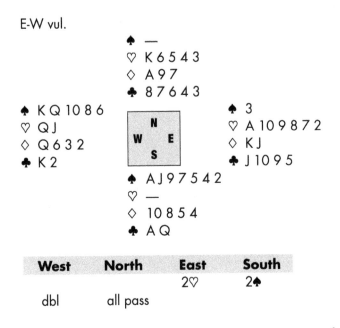

West	North	East	South
		2♡	2♠
dbl	all pass		

East really should have the ♡J instead of the ♡2, but his 9 HCP, good intermediates and two-suited hand make this an acceptable vulnerable preempt. The only suspect bid at the table really belongs to South, and he got caught. Especially since he is on the light side for his bid, South's spade suit should have better texture: ♠AJ10987 keeps South out of hot water.

West is not asking East for a second suit: the double is a penalty double. West knows that South has overcalled a poor suit, which suggests heart shortness — another indicator to defend rather than try to play the hand, even with a known 6-2 heart fit. Here East-West will get four spades, two diamonds and one club for a gain of 300, while nine tricks is the limit in a heart contract.

PART 2

ADVANCED PREEMPTS

Chapter Five

Preempting Partner

When a player preempts in first or second seat, he is hoping that the opponents have the high cards not partner. If he knew partner had a good hand, he would pass and give his partner an unimpeded auction. No question. Since he cannot possibly know whether his partner does have a good hand, the best he can do, in first or second seat, is to preempt properly. This means preempting with a good suit, no void, no four-card major and little outside defense so partner is more likely to do the right thing when he has high cards.

By the same logic, when partner has opened, responder only preempts with very specific hands — the weak jump shift, the inverted minor double raise and the raise of partner's major to the four-level. However, even then it can lead to difficulties:

Example 5.1   North Has More to Say

N-S vul.

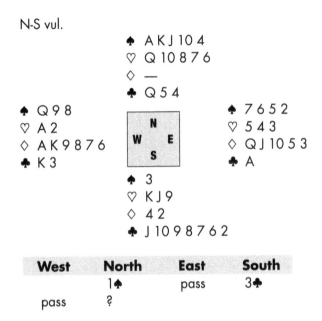

West	North	East	South
	1♠	pass	3♣
pass	?		

What North does now will depend on their exact agreement regarding the 3♣ preempt. Does North risk a 3♡ bid with a club fit? Would he even consider raising clubs? Probably he will leave partner in 3♣, and the heart game will be missed. Of course, if West decides to enter the auction, North-South may still find 4♡.

In this last example, North opened 1♠ and his partner had a weak hand with long clubs. Nevertheless, the response should not be 3♣. Never. Partner may have a big hand and he may be preempted out of the auction not knowing whether or how to proceed. Furthermore, being stranded at the three-level in a double misfit is something to avoid. The following examples show how such a hand should be bid.

Example 5.2 The One Notrump Response has a Purpose

Both vul.

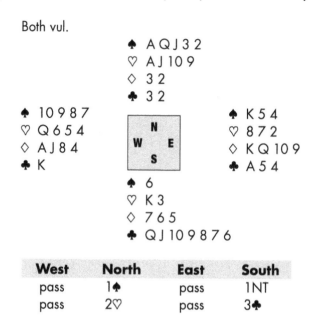

West	North	East	South
pass	1♠	pass	1NT
pass	2♡	pass	3♣

This is how South shows a weak hand with a long club suit in either Standard American or Two-Over-One — it doesn't matter whether the 1NT is forcing or not. It has given opener a chance to describe his hand better than over an immediate jump to 3♣. The key to this bidding sequence is that if partner rebids spades, he can be left in 2♠.

Example 5.1 should also be bid this way, otherwise they might get to 5♣ with no play. In Two-Over-One, a jump to 3♣ (if not a Bergen raise or a minisplinter) can be used as invitational with a reasonable six-card club suit denying spade support.

Example 5.3 Using a Negative Double

N-S vul.

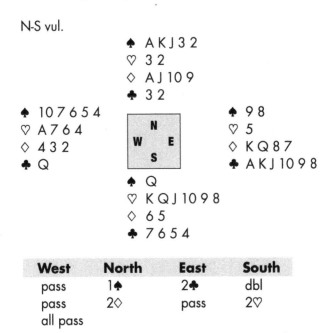

West	North	East	South
pass	1♠	2♣	dbl
pass	2◇	pass	2♡
all pass			

A new suit at the two-level, in competition, is 10+ HCP and promises a re-bid. However, if the new suit bid is preceded by a negative double then it is a weaker hand. When South makes a negative double here he is ostensibly promising the unbid suits, but correcting 2◇ to 2♡ shows a single-suited hand with 6-9 points. If South had 10 HCP and five or more hearts, he would have bid 2♡ directly.

WEAK JUMP SHIFTS

We've seen that jumping to the three-level over partner's opening bid on a weak hand is not a good idea. Weak jump shifts are normally to the two-level. You do not want to jump to the three-level opposite an unlimited partner and end up in a misfit. A weak jump shift is usually a bid of two of a major over one of a minor. (If mini-splinters are not being used, then 2♠ over 1♡ is also weak). A typical hand is 0-4 HCP, and an aceless hand.

Partner opens 1♣. What do you bid with the following?

a)   ♠ 10 9 8 7 6 2 ♡ 7 6 5 ◇ 8 7 6 ♣ 3
b)   ♠ A 10 7 5 3 2 ♡ 7 6 5 ◇ 9 7 ♣ 3 2
c)   ♠ A J 10 9 8 7 ♡ 7 6 5 ◇ 9 7 ♣ 3 2

d) ♠ 1098763 ♡ A72 ◊ 9 ♣ J76
e) ♠ KJ7654 ♡ 765 ◊ 9 ♣ J76
f) ♠ KJ10987 ♡ J32 ◊ 9 ♣ 876
g) ♠ 1076532 ♡ K32 ◊ J ♣ J76

Hand (a) is a clear 2♠ bid. Weak jump shifts do not follow the suit qual-ity rules of a preempt, and the bid is not lead-directing. This weak hand gets entries with spades as trumps, and makes things more difficult for the opponents.

Weak jump shifts usually deny an ace, so (b), (c) and (d) are all 1♠ responses.

In (e) and (f), four points in the long suit are gold and make the hand worth a 1♠ response. However, the wasted points in (g) make it a weak jump shift to 2♠.

Example 5.4   Partner Needs a Lot to Raise a Weak Jump Shift

Neither vul.

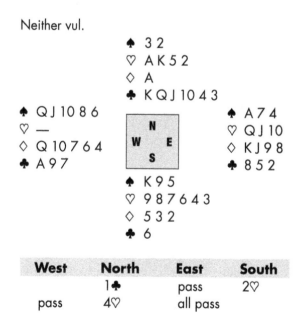

West	North	East	South
	1♣	pass	2♡
pass	4♡	all pass	

There are many 17-point hands that do not take action over a partner's weak jump shift. However, here North can count tricks in the form of los-ers. He has only three losers if AKxx takes care of a six-card trump suit, and therefore he can bid 4♡. As it turns out, declarer loses one spade, one heart, no diamonds and one club for +420. In general, a hand that raises a weak jump shift to game is either distributional or likely a 2NT opener or better.

You open 1♣. What do you bid over partner's 2♠ (WJS) with the following hands?

a) ♠ A J ♡ A K 5 4 ◇ K J 10 ♣ K J 10 9
b) ♠ A J 3 ♡ A Q 5 ◇ K J 10 ♣ K J 10 9
c) ♠ 8 7 ♡ A K Q 3 ◇ 9 7 2 ♣ A K Q 2
d) ♠ A K ♡ A K 2 ◇ 9 3 2 ♣ A 7 6 3 2
e) ♠ A K 3 2 ♡ A K 2 ◇ 9 3 2 ♣ A J 3
f) ♠ A 5 3 2 ♡ A K 2 ◇ 9 ♣ A K 10 9 8

Hand (a) is very marginal but there are two sure minor-suit losers (and likely more) along with probable spade losers, so a pass is indicated. Look at hands (a) and (g) in the previous quiz and ask yourself whether you want to be in 4♠ opposite those.

Hand (b) is similar to (a), but even though the trump suit might only have one loser, I would still pass. With (c), the pointed suits will lead to enough losers to bid no higher. With (d), the minors will lead to three or four losers and you have a probable trump loser too.

Hand (e) is very close to a raise, but there may be four minor-suit losers. At matchpoints, when in doubt, get a positive score, so pass. Vulnerable at teams, bid 4♠. By contrast, hand (f) can likely cover all but two or three losers, so 4♠ is very likely to succeed and you should bid it.

These examples show that counting points in these auctions is not as effective as counting losers.

RESPONDING TO A TAKEOUT DOUBLE

So far, we have looked at situations where partner has opened and you hold a long suit. How about opposite a takeout double? In response to a takeout double, if RHO passes, you must bid, however weak your hand. A pass shows enough values to penalize the opponent.

West	North	East	South
1♣	dbl	pass	1♠

Here, 1♠ is the weakest response, not 2♠ or 3♠. You do not want to pre-empt partner when he is known to have an opener. A jump to 2♠ is 9 to a bad 12. A full opening response is the cuebid. A response of 3♠ can be played in various ways — Mike Lawrence suggests about 6-8 points but with good playing strength. Discuss this with your partner.

Example 5.5   A Jump is Not Weak

N-S vul.

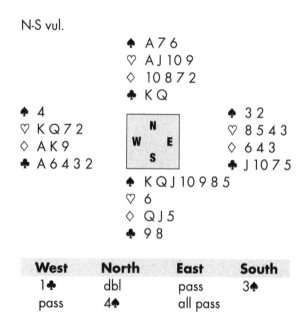

West	North	East	South
1♣	dbl	pass	3♠
pass	4♠	all pass	

North decides to double rather than overcall 1NT with only one club stopper. Now South has a 'picture bid' available with 3♠. North has a little extra and accepts the invite. However, if West opens 1◊, North should not make a minimum off-shape double, especially vulnerable, so the bidding should go as follows.

West	North	East	South
1◊	pass	pass	3♠
all pass			

South is perfectly fine preempting the auction when his partner is a passed hand. South loses three tricks and makes +620 in either case.

INVERTED MINORS

The disadvantage of inverted minors is that sometimes a player just does not want to go to the three-level with a weak hand. Sometimes, a player would rather be able to use a simple raise as 6 to 9 in an attempt to get a positive score.

Example 5.6   The Three-Level is Too High to Get a Plus Score

The following example is from my Kootenay Jewel bridge club in Warfield, BC.

N-S vul.

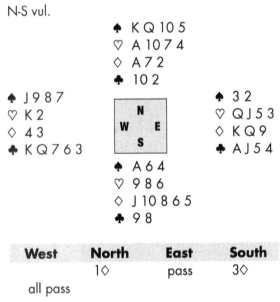

West	North	East	South
	1◇	pass	3◇
all pass			

North-South were playing inverted minors, and South's jump to 3◇ showed a weak hand and no four-card major. Unfortunately, 3◇ went down two for -200, a poor matchpoint result against 110 the other way. South was perhaps unlucky to find only three trumps opposite, but perhaps his good intermediates and balanced shape should have suggested a 1NT bid at this vulnerability. Don't be a slave to system — there are other factors to consider too.

JUMPS IN COMPETITIVE AUCTIONS

The basic principle of competitive auctions is to obstruct the communication between the opponents. A player must bid the limit of his hand immediately and give the opponents the last guess.

Example 5.7   Bid the Limit of the Hand Right Away

Neither vul.

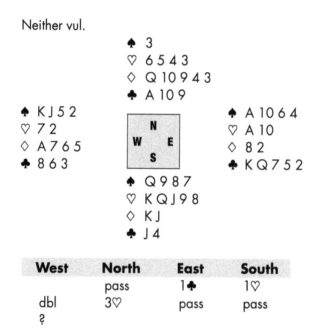

West	North	East	South
	pass	1♣	1♡
dbl	3♡	pass	pass
?			

The opponents asked, 'Is 3♡ preemptive?'

Well, three people have some high cards, and North has what little is left over. Here, North is following the Law and has four hearts — if he had bid 2♡, he planned on bidding 3♡ over 2♠. Therefore he did it right away, giving the last guess to the opponents. If East bids 3♠, he is implying a bigger hand than he has — but he may just be under pressure, so West doesn't know whether to go on or not. Here, West does not know if East passed because he is a minimum or because he does not have four spades. West clearly does not have enough to double again, so he must pass.

The situation is completely different if North only bids 2♡:

West	North	East	South
	pass	1♣	1♡
dbl	2♡	2♠	pass
pass	3♡	pass	pass
3♠	all pass		

East can bid 2♠ because he is only making a simple raise of West's virtual 1♠ bid. West can pass, and when North bids 3♡ he can come back in with 3♠ and East knows it is not an invitation. On a club lead, 3♡ makes for +140, so even if 3♠ goes down, as it may, -50 is better than -140.

Chapter Six

Avoiding Self-Preempts

All preemptive hands are 10 points or fewer, but they also cannot make game opposite a minimum opener held by a partner. The biggest problem people have with evaluating hands with long suits, is that HCP are not that accurate — it is tricks that should be counted.

Consider the following two hands.

♠ K Q 10 8 6 5 4 2   ♡ 7   ◇ A J 8 7   ♣ —   4 losers

♠ K Q 10 8 6 5 4 2   ♡ 7 2   ◇ 8 7   ♣ 7   6 losers

They cannot be represented by the same bid. Agreed? Counting losers is the same as counting tricks. The number of tricks is just thirteen minus the number of losers.

Example 6.1 What is Weak?

E-W vul.

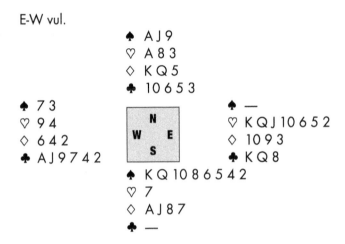

```
              ♠ A J 9
              ♡ A 8 3
              ◇ K Q 5
              ♣ 10 6 5 3
♠ 7 3                          ♠ —
♡ 9 4          N              ♡ K Q J 10 6 5 2
◇ 6 4 2     W     E           ◇ 10 9 3
♣ A J 9 7 4 2   S            ♣ K Q 8
              ♠ K Q 10 8 6 5 4 2
              ♡ 7
              ◇ A J 8 7
              ♣ —
```

This is a very interesting deal. Neither South nor East have preemptive hands. A preempt by East is rather fortunate, and works out well because his partner turns out to have very few high cards. However, my real point is that no score higher than 510 was achieved North-South at my Kootenay Jewel bridge club. Every South preempted to 4♠. Here is the proper bidding.

West	North	East	South
		1♡	dbl
pass	2♡	pass	2♠
pass	3♣	pass	5♣
pass	5♠	pass	6◇
pass	7♠	all pass	

North cuebids to show an opener and the game force is on. South shows a spade suit, and North raises. Now 5♣ is Exclusion Blackwood, and 5♠ shows two keycards outside clubs without the ♠Q. Now South can try for seven with 6◇, promising all of the keycards and asking for second- and third-round control in diamonds. North has both second- and third-round diamond controls and just bids 7♠. I'm not suggesting it's necessarily easy to get to the grand slam, but surely one pair should have reached 6♠ at least!

Example 6.2 A Preempt Cannot Be a Bid of Strength

This hand occurred during the penultimate round of the team event of a Cranbrook sectional. North guessed correctly that 6◊ was being bid to make not to preempt the auction for a passed hand opposite a third-seat opener.

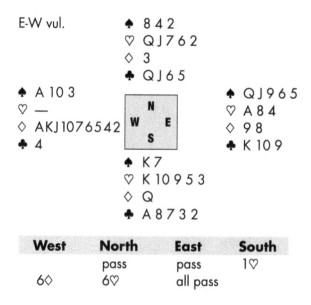

E-W vul.

```
              ♠ 8 4 2
              ♡ Q J 7 6 2
              ◊ 3
              ♣ Q J 6 5

♠ A 10 3                      ♠ Q J 9 6 5
♡ —                          ♡ A 8 4
◊ A K J 10 7 6 5 4 2         ◊ 9 8
♣ 4                          ♣ K 10 9

              ♠ K 7
              ♡ K 10 9 5 3
              ◊ Q
              ♣ A 8 7 3 2
```

West	North	East	South
	pass	pass	1♡
6◊	6♡	all pass	

At the other table, the bidding went as follows:

West	North	East	South
	pass	pass	1♡
5◊	5♡	all pass	

At both tables, the contract was undoubled and set by three tricks, so this bizarre board was a push. Both West players decided to lie about their hand. What would West bid with the following hand?

$$♠ 10\ 3 \quad ♡ 3 \quad ◊ K Q J 10 7 6 5 4 2 \quad ♣ 4 \qquad \text{5 losers}$$

How can East tell the difference? That five-loser hand is a preempt, while the actual three-loser hand is certainly not. (A nine-card suit to the AK can surely be counted for no losers.) West cannot treat his hand as a preempt, or the opponents will end up playing undoubled. The bidding should go as follows:

West	North	East	South
	pass	pass	1♡
dbl	4♡	4♠	pass
6◇	all pass		

East shows stuff by bidding over 4♡ and West can bid 6◇, this time after a double. Now, North can still come back into this auction, but he will be doubled. If 6♡ is properly defended, that would be down four for -800, quite a bit better than giving up 1370, but still a loss of 11 IMPs. Yes, 6♡ was a good bid even if doubled as it should have been. Only North guessed what was happening, luckily enough. A key principle is illustrated here. Whether preempting the auction or responding to a partner's takeout double, *a strong hand cannot make the same bid a weak hand would or could.* Perhaps, if partner is known to have nothing, any sort of preempt can be made without giving partner difficulties as long as the suit is of good enough quality to draw trumps quickly and to be a good lead-direct.

Example 6.3 Two-suited Hands Are Stronger than the Point Count Indicates

A problem that arises with a preempt being too strong is when the hand is two-suited or contains a void. Even a minimum 5-5 hand will make game opposite a four-card limit raise. Hands with 6-4 shape are also powerful, and 6-5 hands ('6-5 come alive') even more so.

Neither vul.

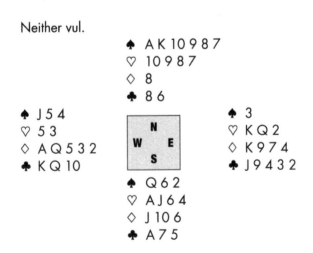

West	North	East	South
	pass	pass	1♣
pass	1♠	pass	1NT
pass	2♡	pass	3♡
pass	4♡	all pass	

North does not open 2♠ because of the outside four-card major and also because the two-suited hand has offensive potential. For the point counters, North-South can make game here with 19 HCP, and South has the flattest hand possible. North-South are playing NMF so 2♡ denies 10 HCP; nevertheless, South raises because of the double fit. The 4-4 fit plays well because losers can go away on the long suit and ruffs can be taken in either hand.

Example 6.4 An Opening Dilemma

A common dilemma between opening 1♠ and preempting 2♠ occurs when a player has six solid cards in a major and nothing outside.

Neither vul.

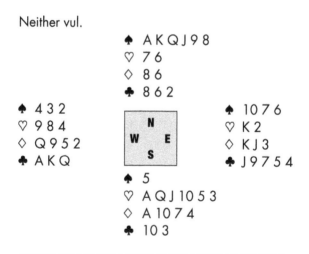

```
              ♠ A K Q J 9 8
              ♡ 7 6
              ◇ 8 6
              ♣ 8 6 2
♠ 4 3 2                        ♠ 10 7 6
♡ 9 8 4          N             ♡ K 2
◇ Q 9 5 2     W     E          ◇ K J 3
♣ A K Q          S             ♣ J 9 7 5 4
              ♠ 5
              ♡ A Q J 10 5 3
              ◇ A 10 7 4
              ♣ 10 3
```

West	North	East	South
	1♠	pass	2♡
pass	2♠	pass	3◇
pass	3♠	pass	4♠
all pass			

Some Norths will open 2♠, which will certainly kill any prospect of game, but I will open 1♠. Here, the spades are strong enough that 4♠ is a reasonable contract — indeed, better than 4♡. Here is a bit of history: in Kaplan and Sheinwold's *The Kaplan-Sheinwold System of Winning Bridge*, any hand with three quick tricks is an opener.

Example 6.5 This Just Has to Be a One-level Opening

Adding another spade to North's hand actually simplifies the situation. With a seven-card suit, I add 3 points to the hand on opening.

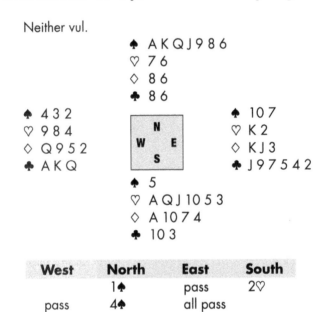

Neither vul.

```
              ♠ A K Q J 9 8 6
              ♡ 7 6
              ◇ 8 6
              ♣ 8 6
♠ 4 3 2                        ♠ 10 7
♡ 9 8 4         N             ♡ K 2
◇ Q 9 5 2    W     E          ◇ K J 3
♣ A K Q         S             ♣ J 9 7 5 4 2
              ♠ 5
              ♡ A Q J 10 5 3
              ◇ A 10 7 4
              ♣ 10 3
```

West	North	East	South
	1♠	pass	2♡
pass	4♠	all pass	

Notice in both examples 6.4 and 6.5, an opening preempt denies an opening bid, and would prevent North-South from reaching game. In both cases 4♠ is a better contract than 4♡. Can you get to 4♠?

Example 6.6 A Preempt Denies the Equivalent to an Opener

This deal is from an ACBL BBO speedball tourney.

N-S vul.

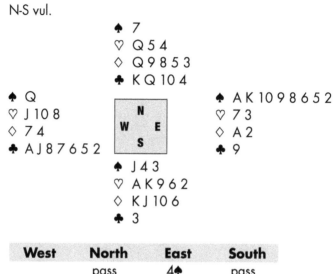

```
                    ♠ 7
                    ♡ Q 5 4
                    ◊ Q 9 8 5 3
                    ♣ K Q 10 4
    ♠ Q                           ♠ A K 10 9 8 6 5 2
    ♡ J 10 8          N           ♡ 7 3
    ◊ 7 4         W       E       ◊ A 2
    ♣ A J 8 7 6 5 2      S        ♣ 9
                    ♠ J 4 3
                    ♡ A K 9 6 2
                    ◊ K J 10 6
                    ♣ 3
```

West	North	East	South
	pass	4♠	pass
pass	4NT	pass	5◊
all pass			

It works out better if West doubles 5◊, but he thought his partner was weak. *A 4♠ opening bid is a weak bid denying an opening hand.* North's 4NT was a good bid made because he thought East was weak, and 5◊ went undoubled because West also thought East was weak.

The bidding should have gone as follows.

West	North	East	South
	pass	1♠	2♡
dbl	pass	4♠	all pass

West makes a negative double, planning to rebid clubs and show a weakish single-suited hand. If North or South venture a five-level bid, they will not get away undoubled.

Namyats

East's hand above is a good example of a hand that is too strong for a normal preempt. A convention called Namyats (Stayman spelled backwards) takes care of stronger preempts with zero- or one-loser seven-card suits and a total of eight or nine playing tricks. Using this method, an opening 4♣ shows hearts, and 4◇ shows spades.

Example 6.7 Preempting with Opening Values Makes Life Difficult

Neither vul.

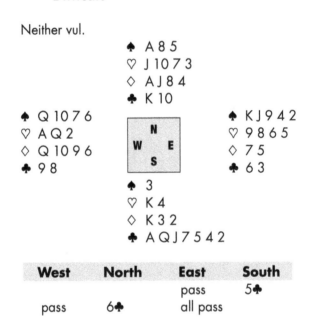

	♠ A 8 5	
	♡ J 10 7 3	
	◇ A J 8 4	
	♣ K 10	

♠ Q 10 7 6		♠ K J 9 4 2
♡ A Q 2		♡ 9 8 6 5
◇ Q 10 9 6		◇ 7 5
♣ 9 8		♣ 6 3

	♠ 3	
	♡ K 4	
	◇ K 3 2	
	♣ A Q J 7 5 4 2	

West	North	East	South
		pass	5♣
pass	6♣	all pass	

Out of twenty-eight tables in an ACBL BBO IMP speedball tourney, three declarers were in 6♣. One made it because West led the ♡A, after which the ♡Q could be ruffed out to pitch a diamond.

This is an example of being preempted by partner who, with three cards total in the majors, feared a major-suit contract by the opponents. He hoped that 5♣ would also discourage partner from attempting a major-suit game. It did. If South opens 1♣, as he should, they can comfortably bid to 5♣ or 3NT, without getting too high.

Can I say it enough? *You do not preempt with an opening hand.* Can I say it any more simply?

Example 6.8 Preempting with a Void and a Four-card Major
— Another No-no

This was a hand that occurred during the Friday midnight Swiss event at a Trail summer sectional.

N-S vul.

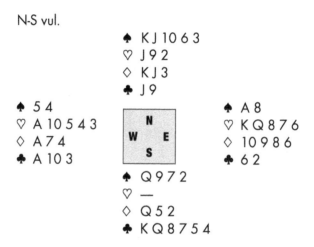

```
                    ♠ K J 10 6 3
                    ♡ J 9 2
                    ◇ K J 3
                    ♣ J 9
  ♠ 5 4                              ♠ A 8
  ♡ A 10 5 4 3         N            ♡ K Q 8 7 6
  ◇ A 7 4          W       E        ◇ 10 9 8 6
  ♣ A 10 3             S            ♣ 6 2
                    ♠ Q 9 7 2
                    ♡ —
                    ◇ Q 5 2
                    ♣ K Q 8 7 5 4
```

At one table, the auction went as follows:

West	North	East	South
		pass	3♣
all pass			

At the other table, the auction was a little different:

West	North	East	South
		pass	pass
1♡	1♠	2♠	4♠
5♡	pass	pass	5♠
all pass			

The first South made a preempt with a void and a four-card major. I do not do this in first or second seat because it is hard to know whether this hand is really weak. Opposite 10 HCP here, South can make 4♠. Therefore, South has a hand better than a bare opener once partner's suit is known to be spades. It is clearly a hand that cannot make a preempt.

However, South was not punished for his poor choice of bids, because an ill-judged 5♠ went down one at the other table. South was not convinced that preempting with a void and a four-card major was wrong: after all, it earned him 5 IMPs.

Example 6.9 1♡ or 4♡ Opening

This board occurred during the first round of the Sunday team event of a Vernon Silver Star sectional. South opened the hand 1♡, and at the other table, the hand was opened 4♡. Not only is South's hand a 1♡ opening, it is a hand that will rebid 4♡. Clearly, a lot of players have trouble with hands with a long suit.

N-S vul.

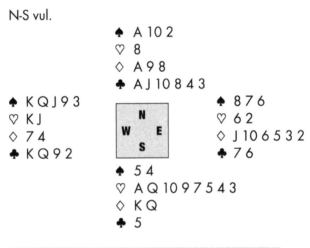

	♠ A 10 2	
	♡ 8	
	◇ A 9 8	
	♣ A J 10 8 4 3	

♠ K Q J 9 3		♠ 8 7 6
♡ K J		♡ 6 2
◇ 7 4		◇ J 10 6 5 3 2
♣ K Q 9 2		♣ 7 6

	♠ 5 4	
	♡ A Q 10 9 7 5 4 3	
	◇ K Q	
	♣ 5	

West	North	East	South
			1♡
1♠	2♣	pass	4♡
pass	6♡	all pass	

At the other table, the bidding went as follows.

West	North	East	South
			4♡
pass	4NT	pass	5♣
pass	5♡	all pass	

This is a perfect example of how South preempted his own side and left his partner guessing about the correct contract. North still almost got to slam, but a little voice kept telling him that his partner had preempted, so he should not push.

Example 6.10 South Preempted Himself Out of a Good Score

Both vul.

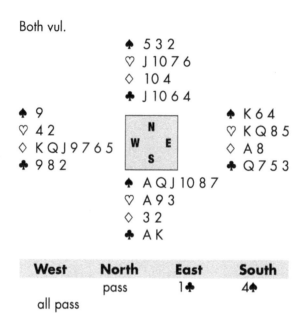

♠ 5 3 2
♡ J 10 7 6
◇ 10 4
♣ J 10 6 4

♠ 9
♡ 4 2
◇ K Q J 9 7 6 5
♣ 9 8 2

♠ K 6 4
♡ K Q 8 5
◇ A 8
♣ Q 7 5 3

♠ A Q J 10 8 7
♡ A 9 3
◇ 3 2
♣ A K

West	North	East	South
	pass	1♣	4♠
all pass			

This was a hand that occurred during a Vernon sectional pair event. Perhaps South had a momentary lapse of reason, although Pink Floyd was not being played. A jump to 4♠ is perhaps a better bid at teams because partner does not need much for game to make. At matchpoints, South should be concerned about just getting a positive score. He went down one in 4♠ for a score of 20%, while +140 would have been a top.

The bidding should go as follows:

West	North	East	South
	pass	1♣	dbl
1◇	pass	pass	1NT
2◇	pass	pass	3♠
all pass			

Chapter Seven

Undisciplined Preempts

I'm not recommending undisciplined preempts, but it must be admitted that sometimes they work well — when the opponents have the high cards and do not double for penalty. Here is a preempt that evoked the wrong response from the opponents, resulting in a top board for the undisciplined preemptor.

Example 7.1   Gotcha, Once More!

N-S vul.

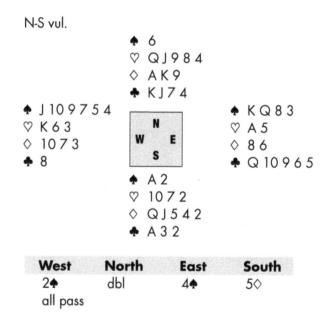

West	North	East	South
2♠	dbl	4♠	5◇
all pass			

South got a zero, because every other West passed, and the other North-South pairs were able to get to 4♡ rather than 5◇.

The worst type of undisciplined preempt is one made on a poor suit, headed by the jack or worse. A suit headed by the queen is not much better, but is more lead-directing than a suit headed by the jack. The test for lead-direction is to imagine that partner has the king doubleton: if the lead of the king does not cost a trick, then the suit is adequate for lead direction.

Yes, I overcall excellent four-card suits at the one-level, have solid two-level overcalls, do not make minimum off-shape takeout doubles, make proper notrump overcalls and certainly disciplined preempts. I am able to do this because I, like my partners, balance fervently when it is correct to do so.

Sometimes bad preempts get good results, while the more common consequential bad results get blamed on bad luck or on the partner. The downside to bad preempts, which happens to be huge, is that partner, if he has a good hand, will never be sure what to do. After all, any beginner can preempt, but only a good player can consistently field good preempts properly. Fielding a preempt that could be bad or good is next to impossible.

Yes, I am an aggressive bidder at matchpoints and when vulnerable games are involved at IMPs, but my preempts are still disciplined. My preempts contain good suits and have little defense on the side, but my weak twos can be five cards as long as I am short in the unbid majors. However, even in third seat, the suit I bid is a suit that I want led, and it is safe for partner to do so.

Example 7.2 Completely Different Hands
Compare the following hands.

$$\spadesuit 4\,3 \quad \heartsuit 3\,2 \quad \diamondsuit 10\,9\,8\,7\,6\,5 \quad \clubsuit A\,K\,3$$
$$\spadesuit 4\,3 \quad \heartsuit 3\,2 \quad \diamondsuit A\,K\,10\,9\,8\,5 \quad \clubsuit 8\,7\,6$$

They have the same points and the same shape, but the first one is never a preempt, even at gunpoint.

Please allow me to repeat for needed emphasis. *For preempts, I insist on good suits with two of the top three honors or three of the top five.* Because the preempt suit is good, there is little room for defensive tricks in side suits, nor do we want to have them. Preempts should be less than 10 points, and opposite a minimum opener from partner, should not expect to make game. This can be tricky because seven-card suits and two-suited hands usually play better than the high-card point totals indicate.

Example 7.3 A Preempt is a Descriptive Bid, and Partner is On Your Team

I play online with a player who plays at lunch in the group that my father used to manage before he retired. This player is good for someone who has not played duplicate, but he has a bit to learn about preempts and his preempts are completely undisciplined.

On one deal, vulnerable versus not, he opened 2◊, in first seat, with the following hand:

♠ 10 9 8 6 4   ♡ 3   ◊ K 10 7 6 3 2   ♣ 8

Opposite a disciplined weak two, I could count nine tricks in notrump opposite my hand, which was:

♠ A 2   ♡ A 7 4 2   ◊ A 5 4   ♣ A 9 5 3

Here, however, 3NT did not fare too well as the diamonds did not run. A little later, we were again vulnerable against not, and partner, in second seat, opened 2♡ with the following hand.

♠ Q 7 6   ♡ A K J 10 7 3   ◊ 8   ♣ 6 3 2

This hand does not even need an opening bid from partner to make game. You will make 4♡ opposite the following hands, among many others, that have less than opening values:

♠ A K 4 3   ♡ Q 9 8 2   ◊ 10 7 5   ♣ 5 4
♠ K J 10 9   ♡ Q 9 8 2   ◊ 10 7 5   ♣ A 4
♠ J 10 9   ♡ Q 9 8 2   ◊ A 7 5 2   ♣ A 4

These are all sub-openers. As stated previously, any hand that makes game opposite an opener is also an opener, but a hand that makes game opposite a sub-opener is better than a minimum opener. So, this hand cannot be a preempt. It is a hand that can open 1♡ and is practically playable in a heart contract even if partner is void.

The bottom line to this example is: how can partner do the right thing when a preempt can have such a huge range in value? Bridge is a partnership game, and preempts must be consistent at a particular vulnerability so that partner can do the right thing. Good preemptors minimize the bad effect on partner while maximizing the difficulty for the opponents.

Preempts can do the following:

- Accurately describe the hand to partner.
- Warn partner to stay out of the bidding with a misfit, a singleton or a void in the preempt suit.
- Suggest a lead.
- Suggest a place to make a sacrifice if partner has little in the way of defensive tricks and a lot in the way of support.

Example 7.4 Lead-direction — the Downside of a Poor Suit

Both vul.

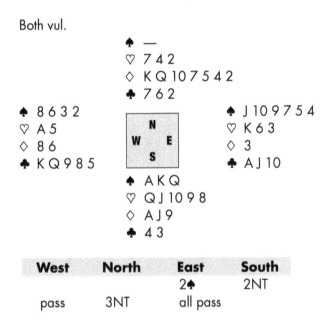

	♠ —	
	♡ 7 4 2	
	◇ K Q 10 7 5 4 2	
	♣ 7 6 2	
♠ 8 6 3 2		♠ J 10 9 7 5 4
♡ A 5	N	♡ K 6 3
◇ 8 6	W E	◇ 3
♣ K Q 9 8 5	S	♣ A J 10
	♠ A K Q	
	♡ Q J 10 9 8	
	◇ A J 9	
	♣ 4 3	

West	North	East	South
		2♠	2NT
pass	3NT	all pass	

Undisciplined preempts sometimes hurt because they get partner off to the wrong lead. West has four spades and two or three side entries. On this auction, he cannot lead anything but a spade. Had East been quiet, as he should have been, West leads a club, and they set the contract by three tricks (five clubs and two hearts). On a spade lead, declarer rattles off ten tricks for +630.

Example 7.5 Punish Them when They Double Partner's Preempt

This board occurred during a BBO IMP speedball tourney. It is an example of how the opponents should be made to pay for stepping into the wrong preemptive auction. I have included the example in this chapter because making a weak two with a seven-card suit is, in principle, undisciplined.

Both vul.

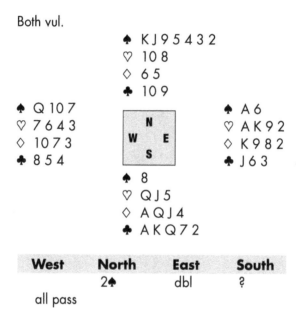

```
                    ♠ K J 9 5 4 3 2
                    ♡ 10 8
                    ◇ 6 5
                    ♣ 10 9
  ♠ Q 10 7                              ♠ A 6
  ♡ 7 6 4 3              N              ♡ A K 9 2
  ◇ 10 7 3          W        E          ◇ K 9 8 2
  ♣ 8 5 4               S              ♣ J 6 3
                    ♠ 8
                    ♡ Q J 5
                    ◇ A Q J 4
                    ♣ A K Q 7 2
```

West	North	East	South
	2♠	dbl	?
all pass			

South, bid 3NT because he was worried 2♠ doubled would be converted to penalty since his partner regularly bids five-card weak twos. After all, South was short in spades, and by definition, the doubler is short in spades. (Right? Please say yes!)

However, South should pass and double wherever they end up. That is likely to reap more rewards than playing a 3NT contract (not to mention that 3NT went down).

The bidding should go as follows:

West	North	East	South
	2♠	dbl	pass
3♡	pass	pass	dbl
all pass			

Even if West passes, partner will likely do well in 2♠ doubled, especially if the spade length is in front of him.

Yes, North opened a weak two with a seven-card suit, so he definitely could withstand a penalty double. After all, partner did choose to make a vulnerable weak two. The seven-card suit somewhat makes up for the weak hand strength, and 7=2=2=2 is not the most attractive shape.

Did you ever notice that a good player salivates when the opponents get into trouble vulnerable?

Example 7.6 Introduction of Uncertainty

Both vul.

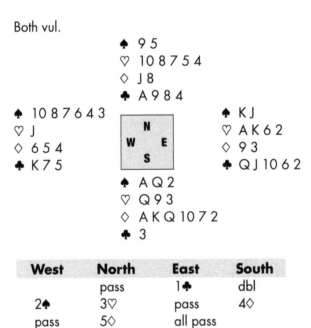

West	North	East	South
	pass	1♣	dbl
2♠	3♡	pass	4◇
pass	5◇	all pass	

This example illustrates how a preempt introduces uncertainty into the auction. I am not a fan of preempting in a suit in which an opponent has implied length, but it worked out well here. Both North-South have to find bids under pressure, with very little space left. Perhaps South should bid 4♡ instead of 4◇, but we can understand his choice. On this layout 4♡ makes, but 5◇ doesn't.

Example 7.7   Pay Attention to Vulnerability

N-S vul.

```
              ♠ A K Q 7 5
              ♡ A Q 9 8 2
              ◇ A
              ♣ 9 2
  ♠ 10 4                        ♠ 9 3
  ♡ 10 6           N            ♡ J 4
  ◇ J 9 7 6 4   W     E         ◇ K Q 10 3 2
  ♣ Q 5 4 3        S            ♣ 10 8 7 6
              ♠ J 8 6 2
              ♡ K 7 5 3
              ◇ 8 5
              ♣ A K J
```

West	North	East	South
		2◇	dbl
4◇	6◇	pass	6♡
all pass			

When the vulnerability favors you, it is more reasonable to breach discipline: after all, there are two opponents who rate to have good hands, and only one partner. This deal occurred during an ACBL matchpoint speedball tourney on BBO. It was played sixty-six times, and only twice did East open 2◇. East chooses to bid a five-card weak two when partner's strength is undisclosed because he does not have three or more cards in a major. He also has a second suit in the other minor which, although it never will be bid, often increases the playability of a contract. Four other times, East passed and then later made a 2◇ overcall.

In one case, West got excited and bid 5◇, which went down five doubled, -1100. That was a good board for West (83.08%) because fifty-four North-South pairs were in slam. Of those fifty-four, eighteen were in a grand, and all of them had an uncontested auction. A loss of 1460 got East-West a surprising 56.15%, partly because 6NT makes the same tricks.

If West bids only 4◇, that will probably disturb the auction enough. However, 4◇ usually does not get played doubled when an opponent is only looking at one or two diamonds. By contrast, the five-level stops the opponents dead in their tracks and, more often than not, they choose to defend a doubled contract.

In this example, it is evident that interference stopped the opponents from finding a pretty easy grand.

Chapter Eight

Cluttered Auctions

If any bridge player were to be asked to imagine a preemptive auction, they would imagine raising partner's preempt to 5♣, giving the opponents 300 instead of 620. However, preempts do not have to be so flashy. Not every weak hand and long suit leads to a sacrifice, but it is still important not to give the opponents all the room they need. Making any auction busy may cause the opponents to misstep. If nothing else, it may prevent the opponents from chalking up an easy plus score.

OVERCALLS

A simple overcall may remove bidding room and put pressure on the opponents, as in the following two auctions.

West	North	East	South
		1♣	1♠

West	North	East	South
		1◊	2♣

So even if a preempt cannot be made, just cluttering the auction with simple overcalls can be effective. An overcall tells partner whether to compete or to defend depending on his length in the overcalled suit. *I consider a third-seat opening also a one-level overcall.* Shortness in the overcall suit tells the partner to stay out of the auction — I hope! What usually happens is that my partner ignores his shortness in my suit, gets into trouble and blames me for not having a good enough opening. At the very least, an overcall will get partner off to the correct lead, assuming good overcalls are the norm. If good overcalls are not the norm, they should be.

One-level overcalls do not need to be lead-directing if they are strong enough. However, all two-level overcalls are lead-directing, usually showing a good six-card suit and 12+ HCP. Any overcall that is not a full opener has to be lead-directing. Four-card one-level overcalls are just good bridge if done with a really strong suit (AKJ10, KQJ10, etc.). A four-card overcall is never a 4-3-3-3 hand and is often made on a four-card major with a weak five-card minor on the side. If the smallest card is the 8 or higher, the suit is likely a candidate for a four-card one-level overcall.

Example 8.1   Sometimes a 1◇ Overcall Causes Confusion

Both vul.

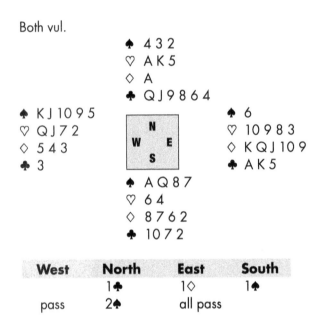

West	North	East	South
	1♣	1◇	1♠
pass	2♣	all pass	

Some people incorrectly believe that South is showing a five-card suit, and equally incorrectly that a double of 1◇ could be made on a hand with 4-3 in the majors. Let their lesson be a bad board. West would love to double for penalty, but his club shortness could be due to North-South having a good fit and a suit to run to. Therefore, he passes and takes his +100.

However, the bidding should go as follows.

West	North	East	South
	1♣	1◇	1♠
pass	2♣	dbl	pass
2♡	pass	pass	3♣
all pass			

North's 3♣ makes +110, which is par on the board.

Example 8.2 Stopper/Negative Double Problem

Both vul.

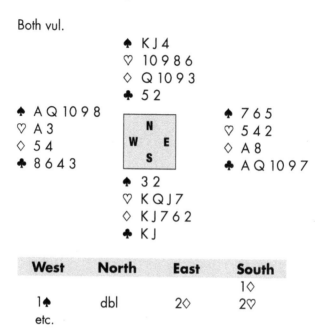

West	North	East	South
			1◊
1♠	dbl	2◊	2♡
etc.			

West has a reasonable one-level overcall with a good suit and an outside control. North's negative double shows one of two types of hands. The first type, as is the case here, shows the unbid suits, especially any unbid major. If South bids clubs, North will correct to diamonds. The second type is a hand with a long suit with less than the 10 HCP needed for a new suit bid at the two-level in competition. Please do not fall into the following bidding trap.

West	North	East	South
			1◊
1♠	1NT	all pass	

One notrump really shows 8-10 HCP, but most importantly, it denies the ability to make a negative double. It also kills any ability to compete. If it turns out that South has a big hand, stoppers always can be shown later, a negative double cannot.

Example 8.3 If West Bids, It Is At the Five-level

E-W vul.

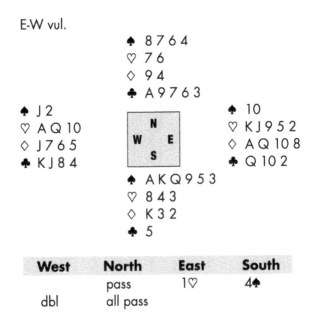

	♠ 8 7 6 4	
	♡ 7 6	
	◇ 9 4	
	♣ A 9 7 6 3	
♠ J 2		♠ 10
♡ A Q 10		♡ K J 9 5 2
◇ J 7 6 5		◇ A Q 10 8
♣ K J 8 4		♣ Q 10 2
	♠ A K Q 9 5 3	
	♡ 8 4 3	
	◇ K 3 2	
	♣ 5	

West	North	East	South
	pass	1♡	4♠
dbl	all pass		

This hand occurred during an ACBL IMP speedball tourney on BBO. South jumped to 4♠, and he gave the last guess to the opponents. Here they were sunk either way — 4♠ makes if they double, and 5♡ goes for 500. South's 4♠ is an excellent bid. The key is to jam the bidding when possible.

Example 8.4   A Phantom Sacrifice

This hand occurred during an ACBL BBO speedball tourney. North is getting into this auction, but it seemed that nobody listened.

Both vul.

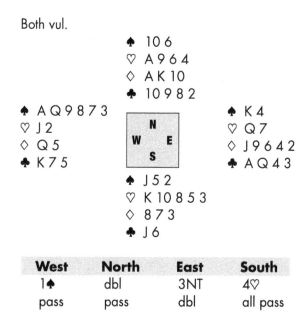

```
                    ♠ 10 6
                    ♡ A 9 6 4
                    ◇ A K 10
                    ♣ 10 9 8 2
    ♠ A Q 9 8 7 3                   ♠ K 4
    ♡ J 2                           ♡ Q 7
    ◇ Q 5                           ◇ J 9 6 4 2
    ♣ K 7 5                         ♣ A Q 4 3
                    ♠ J 5 2
                    ♡ K 10 8 5 3
                    ◇ 8 7 3
                    ♣ J 6
```

West	North	East	South
1♠	dbl	3NT	4♡
pass	pass	dbl	all pass

Sometimes a preempt is not even needed, but a busy auction pressures a player into making the wrong choice. Here, East panicked and bid 3NT without a heart stopper. Did he really think North had no heart suit for his double? South did not realize that the cluttered auction had worked. He obviously felt he was being talked out of something, and decided to convert his comfortable plus into a minus. This is what is called a *phantom sacrifice*. South had no defense outside the heart suit, but he did have one trick, and North had three. North had a light double but not every opening hand has three quick tricks.

A phantom sacrifice is different from a bad sacrifice, which is one that just gives the opponents too large a penalty. More examples are given in Chapter 10.

Example 8.5   A Cluttered Auction

This deal occurred happened during KO Teams at a Victoria regional tournament. It illustrates how an opponent opened 1♠ with a ten-count, nothing abnormal for third seat, but provided difficulties for North-South. The auction was not jammed, just a little cluttered.

Both vul.

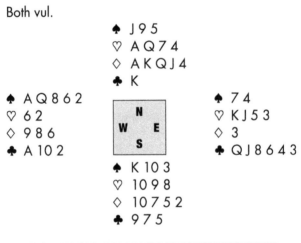

♠ J 9 5
♡ A Q 7 4
◇ A K Q J 4
♣ K

♠ A Q 8 6 2
♡ 6 2
◇ 9 8 6
♣ A 10 2

♠ 7 4
♡ K J 5 3
◇ 3
♣ Q J 8 6 4 3

♠ K 10 3
♡ 10 9 8
◇ 10 7 5 2
♣ 9 7 5

West	North	East	South
		pass	pass
1♠	dbl	pass	2◇
pass	2♠	pass	2NT
pass	3NT	all pass	

South must always bid 2NT because he has a stopper that his partner was requesting. However, when the smoke clears, he is vulnerable in a hopeless contract. The lesson from this deal is that third-seat openings can clutter the auction, and as long as they are lead-directing, I assume partner has the same values as a one-level overcall.

Example 8.6 Four-card Major in Third Seat

Both vul.

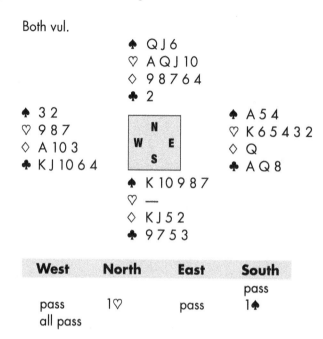

```
              ♠ Q J 6
              ♡ A Q J 10
              ◇ 9 8 7 6 4
              ♣ 2
  ♠ 3 2                        ♠ A 5 4
  ♡ 9 8 7          N           ♡ K 6 5 4 3 2
  ◇ A 10 3      W     E        ◇ Q
  ♣ K J 10 6 4     S           ♣ A Q 8
              ♠ K 10 9 8 7
              ♡ —
              ◇ K J 5 2
              ♣ 9 7 5 3
```

West	North	East	South
			pass
pass	1♡	pass	1♠
all pass			

This deal occurred at a sectional in Spokane, WA. North opens a pretty good four-card heart suit in third seat, and steals his opponents' best fit. When North picks up his hand, he thinks hearts not diamonds, right? He wants hearts led, not diamonds. If partner is ever concerned about a fifth heart, put the ◇6 with the hearts when you put the hand down as dummy.

East has nothing to say. The heart suit is dead with five hearts likely to his right, and the five smallest hearts, in front of his face, tell him to defend. West might have ventured a 2♣ bid if he were in the passout seat. North, by passing 1♠, shows exactly three-card support and probably a sub-opener.

Example 8.7 The Four-card One-level Overcall

I often find that I need to play the cards well to escape from sticky situations that I get into because of aggressive bidding. Nevertheless, you should not be afraid of overcalling a good four-card suit, as in the example below.

Both vul.

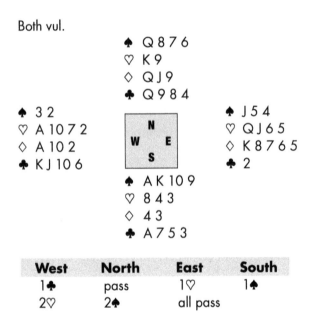

```
              ♠ Q 8 7 6
              ♡ K 9
              ◇ Q J 9
              ♣ Q 9 8 4
♠ 3 2                          ♠ J 5 4
♡ A 10 7 2         N          ♡ Q J 6 5
◇ A 10 2       W     E        ◇ K 8 7 6 5
♣ K J 10 6         S          ♣ 2
              ♠ A K 10 9
              ♡ 8 4 3
              ◇ 4 3
              ♣ A 7 5 3
```

West	North	East	South
1♣	pass	1♡	1♠
2♡	2♠	all pass	

If South does not make a one-level overcall, the bidding will go as follows.

West	North	East	South
1♣	pass	1♡	pass
2♡	pass	pass	?

Now South has a problem. He is short in the unbid diamond suit so he cannot double, and it is more dangerous to balance with a four-card suit at the two-level. A player should never delay a bid just because he thinks the bid is questionable. It should be bid right away or not at all. Now do you see the logic of a four-card one-level overcall? It is way better than a minimum off-shape takeout double.

Example 8.8   Cluttering a Precision 1♣ Auction

I am currently learning a strong club system with canapé bids that my partner calls Bangladesh Blue. I have also played many versions of Precision over the years. Therefore, I know from personal experience how important it is to interfere with a 1♣ auction. Get a good suit mentioned in the auction to get a lead and perhaps a raise from partner.

E-W vul.

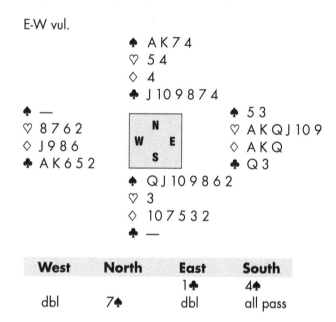

```
              ♠ A K 7 4
              ♡ 5 4
              ◇ 4
              ♣ J 10 9 8 7 4
♠ —                              ♠ 5 3
♡ 8 7 6 2          N            ♡ A K Q J 10 9
◇ J 9 8 6      W       E        ◇ A K Q
♣ A K 6 5 2        S            ♣ Q 3
              ♠ Q J 10 9 8 6 2
              ♡ 3
              ◇ 10 7 5 3 2
              ♣ —
```

West	North	East	South
		1♣	4♠
dbl	7♣	dbl	all pass

This is an extreme example, but when an opponent opens a Precision 1♣, the goal is to see how high you can get the opponents without their exchanging any information about suits. West's double just shows values. In fact, here, East-West can make 7♡ for 2210, but have to settle for +300.

Example 8.9 A Preempt Will Teach a Player Not to Open a Two-suited Hand 2♣

This example is similar to the previous one except this time, a 2♣ opener has been preempted to a high level without a single suit shown. My competitive bidding workshops always have a similar example, and there seems to be an invisible ceiling that prevents all my students preempting higher than 4♠.

N-S vul.

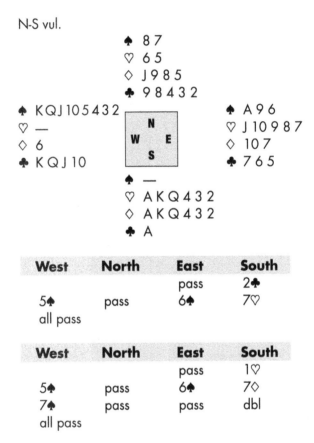

West	North	East	South
		pass	2♣
5♠	pass	6♠	7♡
all pass			

West	North	East	South
		pass	1♡
5♠	pass	6♠	7♢
7♠	pass	pass	dbl
all pass			

Which auction would you prefer? South has an obligation to anticipate what could happen. Should he be surprised that an opponent could preempt in a black suit?

Here, 6♠ goes down one and 7♠ is down two; meanwhile 7◊ makes, and 7♡ is down two. In the first auction, South had to guess at the seven-level, and guessed wrong. The lesson here is that a player should not open 2♣ with a strong two-suited hand. I would love to give this deal to a room full of players and see the huge range of results: from -850 to +1440 or maybe even +2240 (5♠ doubled making to 7◊ redoubled making).

This example and the previous one could be in the sacrifice chapter, but they are extreme examples of cluttered auctions that severely limit the opponents' bidding.

INTERFERING WITH NOTRUMP

Overcalling a notrump opening bid is often more effective than overcalling a suit opening. Players strive to open one notrump as much as possible because bidding is usually easier. Therefore, it is incumbent on the opponents to interfere as much as it is safe to do so. When opponents interfere over a notrump opening, the following may occur:

- The strong hand may become dummy.
- Parts of the bidding system, such as invitational bids, are lost.
- The defense knows which suit to attack.
- The notrump opener and partner may be unsure about stoppers.
- Some method such as Lebensohl becomes necessary — an added complication that could be forgotten or not known correctly.

The penalty double is the best defense against interference. The partner of the notrump opener, when in doubt, should defer to the penalty double with four good cards in the opponent's suit and 5 or more points. The overcaller may be in a misfit situation, and at the very least, dummy entries will be scarce. Therefore, the doubler will usually get what he needs. For this reason, stolen bid doubles except over 2♣ are forbidden. To overcall notrump safely, you need an interference system that shows two-suited hands as well as single-suited hands. It is safer to intervene with two suits.

Example 8.10 Interference Over 1NT Often Reaps Reward

If this example is too much to read, just remember one thing: *you must interfere with one notrump as much as is safely possible using a system that shows two-suited hands.*

N-S vul.

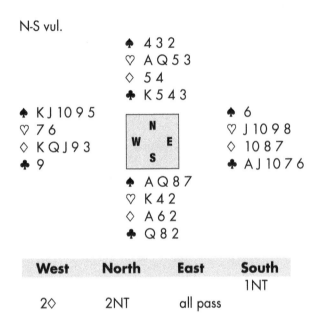

			♠ 4 3 2		
			♡ A Q 5 3		
			◇ 5 4		
			♣ K 5 4 3		

♠ K J 10 9 5   ♠ 6
♡ 7 6   ♡ J 10 9 8
◇ K Q J 9 3   ◇ 10 8 7
♣ 9   ♣ A J 10 7 6

         ♠ A Q 8 7
         ♡ K 4 2
         ◇ A 6 2
         ♣ Q 8 2

West	North	East	South
			1NT
2◇	2NT	all pass	

West must compete if humanly possible. There are many methods that allow you to show two-suited hands as well as one-suited hands. I like Meckwell (modified DONT) the best, but DONT is satisfactory and more common. Everybody knows that competition is bad for the notrump opener, as long as the overcaller does not get heavily penalized. If somebody overcalls a bad suit, they may escape being doubled, but could still get a zero because partner gets off to a costly lead. Here, 2◇ is DONT, showing diamonds and a major.

Lebensohl uses negative doubles at the three-level, however this example shows that negative doubles are needed at the two-level as well, otherwise invitational Stayman is lost. Actually, unless Lebensohl is played, all invitational bids except 2NT are lost. Playing Lebensohl, the invitational 2NT is lost, but other invitational bids are not.

On this deal North may choose to bid 3◇ as game-forcing Stayman with only 9 HCP or as here, he may bid 2NT as invitational, possibly losing a major-suit fit. If partner shows spades over 3◇, North-South are in 3NT with 24 HCP. Therefore, North chooses 2NT, which is where they play — right on this occasion, but you can easily imagine South hands where you want to be in 4♡.

Example 8.11 Balancing Over 1NT

When the bidding goes 1NT-Pass-Pass, you know that your partner is unlikely to lead your longest suit. The more points you hold in that suit, the more likely partner's lead in another suit will cost a trick or two. It really is very imperative to interfere to stop declarer from racking up 150 or more. Again, it is important to have a way to show two- or one-suited hands. High cards are of lesser concern — the cards you do not have, partner will have behind the one-notrump opener. Having a ruffing ability takes priority over points. 'This hand would be nice if I could find the right trump suit,' is what a player who balances over 1NT is likely thinking.

N-S vul.

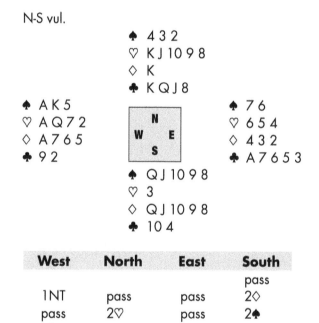

	♠ 4 3 2		
	♡ K J 10 9 8		
	◇ K		
	♣ K Q J 8		

♠ A K 5		♠ 7 6
♡ A Q 7 2		♡ 6 5 4
◇ A 7 6 5		◇ 4 3 2
♣ 9 2		♣ A 7 6 5 3

	♠ Q J 10 9 8		
	♡ 3		
	◇ Q J 10 9 8		
	♣ 10 4		

West	North	East	South
			pass
1NT	pass	pass	2◇
pass	2♡	pass	2♠
all pass			

It is extremely important for South to come into this auction at unfavorable vulnerability. If North-South can make anything, then to get a score defending 1NT, declarer has to be down three in 1NT. However, when the 1NT opener is vulnerable, coming into the auction may save declarer from down two, +200, the goal of all notrump defenders. At the above vulnerability, West's being down two means a profit of only 100 for North-South. West will be down two if North does not lead a heart. In 2♠, because of the heart stoppers in the North hand, the defense cannot tap declarer, who will lose five tricks making +110.

Example 8.12 Penalize as Much as Possible

E-W vul.

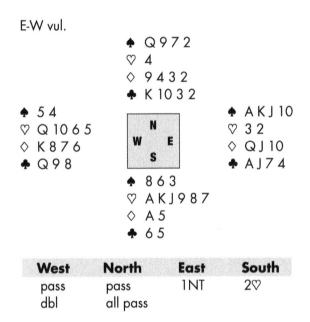

West	North	East	South
pass	pass	1NT	2♡
dbl	all pass		

South will lose three spades, two hearts, one diamond and two clubs for down three and a loss of 500 on a partscore deal. Almost any time an opponent plays doubled in a misfit, the defenders will do better than if they had played their own contract.

Example 8.13 Interference Pushes Opponents to an Unbiddable Game

I suggest playing Lebensohl over interference. It minimizes the number of bids that are lost with interference.

E-W vul.

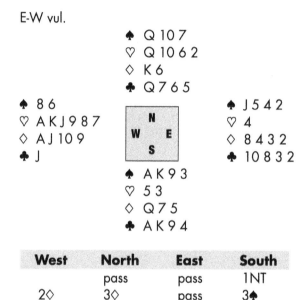

	♠ Q 10 7		
	♡ Q 10 6 2		
	◇ K 6		
	♣ Q 7 6 5		

♠ 8 6   ♠ J 5 4 2
♡ A K J 9 8 7   ♡ 4
◇ A J 10 9   ◇ 8 4 3 2
♣ J   ♣ 10 8 3 2

♠ A K 9 3
♡ 5 3
◇ Q 7 5
♣ A K 9 4

West	North	East	South
	pass	pass	1NT
2◇	3◇	pass	3♠
pass	3NT	all pass	

West uses DONT and bids 2◇ showing diamonds and a higher suit. If Lebensohl is not being used, North can bid 2NT as invitational, but a major fit may be missed. However, North grabs the bull by the horns and forces to game with his 9-count and two tens. South shows a spade suit, and North bids 3NT.

The downside of interference now becomes evident: declarer knows a lot about the distribution, and will use this to bring home a pushy game. Interference gave North a problem to solve, and he decided to go to game with 9 points. He was fortunate that it worked out this time. Any time you make an opponent guess, it will sometimes work in their favor, but my preference is that they are always guessing.

Example 8.14 Interference Leads to Killer Defense

Even over a 1NT opening, interference has lead-direction value, as overcaller does not always end up as declarer.

N-S vul.

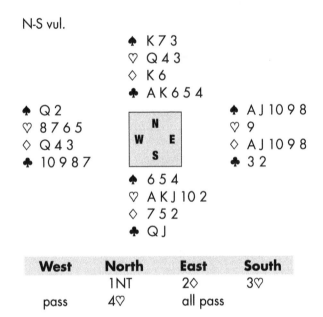

```
              ♠ K 7 3
              ♡ Q 4 3
              ◇ K 6
              ♣ A K 6 5 4
♠ Q 2                          ♠ A J 10 9 8
♡ 8 7 6 5          N           ♡ 9
◇ Q 4 3        W     E         ◇ A J 10 9 8
♣ 10 9 8 7         S           ♣ 3 2
              ♠ 6 5 4
              ♡ A K J 10 2
              ◇ 7 5 2
              ♣ Q J
```

West	North	East	South
	1NT	2◇	3♡
pass	4♡	all pass	

If South has hearts then East's two suits (DONT) are the pointed suits, spades and diamonds. West makes a killer lead of the ♠Q. He ruffs the third spade and puts the ◇Q on the table. Declarer loses five tricks for down two.

North made a fatal mistake by bidding 4♡. Some pairs cannot play notrump with a major fit, but North needs to play 3NT to protect his pointed-suit kings. Depending on the lead, he will make ten or eleven tricks.

TWO-SUITED PREEMPTS

In the previous section, I showed how a system is needed to show two-suited hands over notrump openings. Two-suited hands are more powerful than the points indicate, and allow you to interfere with a modicum of safety. The same holds true when an opponent opens a suit. A cuebid, usually direct and certainly when partner is not involved in the auction, shows a two-suited hand. It is usually Michaels or less frequently, 'top and other'. When partner has done more than pass, cuebids have entirely different meanings.

Michaels Cuebids

West	North	East	South
1♣	2♣		

West	North	East	South
1◇	2◇		

West	North	East	South
1♡	2♡		

West	North	East	South
1♠	2♠		

A cuebid over a minor opening shows the majors, 5-5 or better. The cuebid over a major opening shows the other major and an unspecified minor (2NT asks for the minor). The suits must be playable opposite a worthless doubleton from partner. Playable suits are QJ1092, AJ1092, KQ1092, A10987, etc. Sometimes, not vulnerable, a couple of intermediate cards may be missing, but when vulnerable, the suits have good honors and all the intermediates. Vulnerable Michaels hands are often 6-5.

Example 8.15 Not Time to Use the Convention

When I started playing on BBO, I ran into many good players who refused to play Michaels or unusual notrump. They had run into too many weaker players using the conventions on 5-5 suits such as ♠98732 ♣106532. A lot of players mistakenly think that any agreement listed on the convention card must be used as much as possible.

The first step to becoming a good player, however, is developing patience. This book emphasizes patience in that a player must wait until the correct hand comes along, whether it is a preempt, a sacrifice or any other competitive bid. If the correct hand does not come along enough, I suggest playing more bridge.

E-W vul.

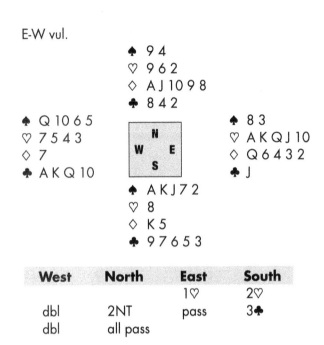

```
                    ♠ 9 4
                    ♡ 9 6 2
                    ◇ A J 10 9 8
                    ♣ 8 4 2
  ♠ Q 10 6 5                        ♠ 8 3
  ♡ 7 5 4 3          N             ♡ A K Q J 10
  ◇ 7           W        E         ◇ Q 6 4 3 2
  ♣ A K Q 10         S             ♣ J
                    ♠ A K J 7 2
                    ♡ 8
                    ◇ K 5
                    ♣ 9 7 6 5 3
```

West	North	East	South
		1♡	2♡
dbl	2NT	pass	3♣
dbl	all pass		

South cuebids hearts showing 5-5 or better in spades and a minor. However, he should not use the convention here as the club suit is not playable. West doubles 2♡ (Anti-Michaels), saying he can penalize at least one of the opponents' suits. North bids 2NT asking for the minor, and South bids clubs. The result: 3♣ doubled is down four for -1100, while 4♡ makes +620. The bidding should go as follows:

West	North	East	South
		1♡	1♠
2♣	pass	4♡	all pass

South has a good 1♠ overcall with a good suit and an outside control. It must be clear that South wants spades led not clubs if he ends up defending. West could make a diamond splinter but devalues the ♠Q. East accepts a limit raise. For North-South, -620 is quite a success compared to -1100. Here, South got into the auction at the one-level and did not commit to a higher and more dangerous level.

Example 8.16 Eight Ever, Nine Ever

E-W vul.

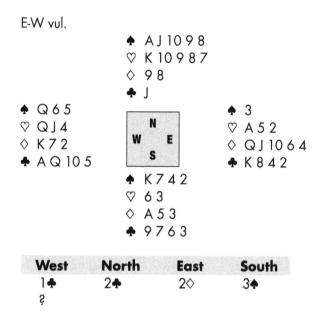

	♠ A J 10 9 8	
	♡ K 10 9 8 7	
	◇ 9 8	
	♣ J	

♠ Q 6 5		♠ 3
♡ Q J 4		♡ A 5 2
◇ K 7 2		◇ Q J 10 6 4
♣ A Q 10 5		♣ K 8 4 2

	♠ K 7 4 2	
	♡ 6 3	
	◇ A 5 3	
	♣ 9 7 6 3	

West	North	East	South
1♣	2♣	2◇	3♠
?			

North makes a Michaels cuebid showing the majors. Once East bids, South can pass if he has nothing. Therefore, 2♠ by South shows something, but a jump to 3♠ obeys the Law.

Now West has a problem. Raising to 4◇ on this rather quacky collection isn't attractive, and notrump might even be the right strain. If he passes, East will not bid again, and South will make eight or nine tricks in spades, depending on how he plays the trump suit. Considering the auction, spades are probably 3-1 and it is more likely that West, who opened, has the ♠Q.

Mini-maxi

I like any two-suited bid to be mostly weak, denying an opening hand. There are other ways to show strong two-suited hands. However, some play 'mini-maxi' which means the Michaels cuebid is either less than an opening hand (mini) or more than 15 HCP (maxi). With a hand in the middle (11-15), you make a simple overcall in the higher-ranking suit.

Example 8.17 Not the Time for Michaels

Neither vul.

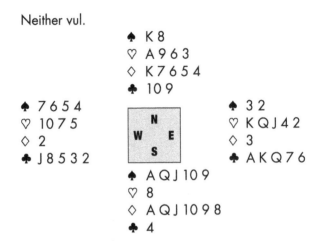

```
                  ♠ K 8
                  ♡ A 9 6 3
                  ◇ K 7 6 5 4
                  ♣ 10 9
  ♠ 7 6 5 4                      ♠ 3 2
  ♡ 10 7 5        N             ♡ K Q J 4 2
  ◇ 2          W     E          ◇ 3
  ♣ J 8 5 3 2      S            ♣ A K Q 7 6
                  ♠ A Q J 10 9
                  ♡ 8
                  ◇ A Q J 10 9 8
                  ♣ 4
```

I strongly prefer Michaels to be weak so I would start bidding the South hand with a double. Sometimes, a hand's strength is distributional not strictly points. South has only four losers. Once North shows some values and a diamond fit, it's easy to get to slam.

Example 8.18 Now Is the Time

Neither vul.

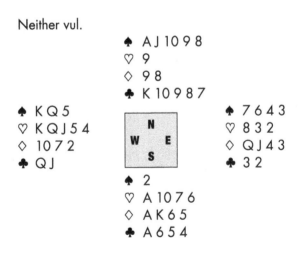

```
                  ♠ A J 10 9 8
                  ♡ 9
                  ◇ 9 8
                  ♣ K 10 9 8 7
  ♠ K Q 5                         ♠ 7 6 4 3
  ♡ K Q J 5 4       N            ♡ 8 3 2
  ◇ 10 7 2       W     E         ◇ Q J 4 3
  ♣ Q J             S            ♣ 3 2
                  ♠ 2
                  ♡ A 10 7 6
                  ◇ A K 6 5
                  ♣ A 6 5 4
```

West	North	East	South
1♡	2♡	pass	2NT
pass	3♣	pass	4♣
pass	4♠	pass	6♣
all pass			

Here, South's club fit and controls in all suits encourage him to try for slam. His 4♣ is a keycard ask, and 4♠ shows two keycards without the ♣Q. South settles for 6♣.

'Top and Other'

This convention is popular in my part of the world. It is the same as Michaels except that a cuebid of a minor shows the top suit, spades, with an unspecified second suit. Combined with the Unusual Notrump, all possible two-suiters can be shown. Many people prefer Michaels because the majors are important. Here is the example that shows why:

Example 8.19 Pass Is Best

Neither vul.

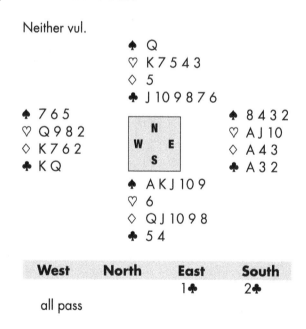

West	North	East	South
		1♣	2♣
all pass			

If 2♣ is Michaels, North will likely bid 4♡; however, South is playing 'top and other'. So, it is likely South's long suits are North's short suits, spades and diamonds. Therefore, he lets his partner play 2♣ and prays the second suit is not hearts. Being realistic, following the percentages and not just hoping for the best, should drive bridge decisions. In general, when you sense a misfit, get out at the lowest level possible.

No, South will not fare well in 2♣, but no one is going to double, and everything else is worse. Playing 'top and other', when a minor is cuebid, any heart contract will be at least at the three-level; if Michaels is used, you can get out in 2♡.

Unusual Notrump for Two Lower Unbid

Unusual notrump is a jump in notrump by an unpassed hand or the cheapest notrump by a passed hand. The unusual notrump commonly shows the two lower unbid suits. Some players play that it always shows both minors even if RHO opened one of them, but this is too restrictive.

West	North	East	South
1◊	2NT		

West	North	East	South
	pass	pass	pass
1◊	1NT		

A jump to 3NT is usually to play whether that was the intention or not. I strive to not throw partner too many curveballs, just maybe a cut fastball or two. The requirements for unusual are the same for Michaels and top and other.

There are many competitive auctions where you have to be alert to realize when a notrump bid is natural, or unusual, or something else entirely.

Example 8.20 No Blackwood and No Quantitative 4NT Here!

Neither vul.

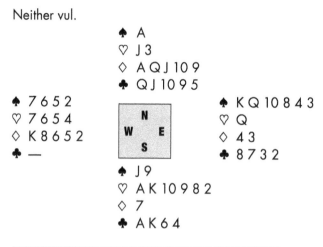

	♠ A	
	♡ J 3	
	◇ A Q J 10 9	
	♣ Q J 10 9 5	

♠ 7 6 5 2		♠ K Q 10 8 4 3
♡ 7 6 5 4		♡ Q
◇ K 8 6 5 2		◇ 4 3
♣ —		♣ 8 7 3 2

	♠ J 9	
	♡ A K 10 9 8 2	
	◇ 7	
	♣ A K 6 4	

West	North	East	South
		2♠	3♡
4♠	4NT	pass	5♣
pass	5◇	pass	5♡
pass	5♠	pass	7♣
all pass			

Here, 4NT is not Blackwood because finding a fit takes priority. Good slam bidding relies on setting trumps and knowing where the tricks are coming from. It is a form of Unusual, showing the two lower unbid suits, in this case, the minors. Now 5♣ agrees trumps, and the rest are cuebids. Both players give their information, and as soon as one player has heard enough, he bids 7♣.

2NT is Not Always Unusual

West	North	East	South
		2♠	2NT

In Chapter 4, I explained why it is bad bridge to preempt a preempt. Nobody should add to the opponent's preempt to further hinder partner. Therefore, any action over a preempt is constructive. So 2NT over an opponent's weak two, in any seat, is the same range as the 1NT direct-seat overcall, about 15-18. Stayman and transfers are on like over 1NT, just one level higher. There are obviously no invitational bids, so if the responder likes his 9-count, he takes the bull by the horns and bids game. I guess this is what bridge players in Pamplona do regularly. Compare the following auction to the previous one:

West	North	East	South
		1♠	2NT

Here, South has the minors and likely a weak hand.

Example 8.21 Not Unusual

Neither vul.

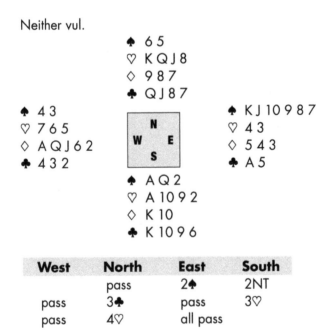

West	North	East	South
	pass	2♠	2NT
pass	3♣	pass	3♥
pass	4♥	all pass	

North has no invitational bid available, so he decides on game with his decent 9 HCP and uses Stayman. It should be obvious that North does not really want to hear whether South has four spades. However, South has four hearts, and North bids game. The spades are positioned nicely, so declarer loses two diamonds and one club for +420.

6-4 Is Not the Same as 5-5

Example 8.22 Six-Four

E-W vul.

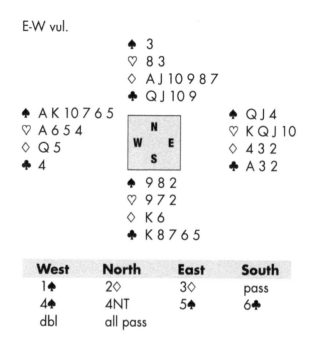

```
                ♠ 3
                ♡ 8 3
                ◊ A J 10 9 8 7
                ♣ Q J 10 9
♠ A K 10 7 6 5                    ♠ Q J 4
♡ A 6 5 4          N              ♡ K Q J 10
◊ Q 5         W       E           ◊ 4 3 2
♣ 4               S              ♣ A 3 2
                ♠ 9 8 2
                ♡ 9 7 2
                ◊ K 6
                ♣ K 8 7 6 5
```

West	North	East	South
1♠	2◊	3◊	pass
4♠	4NT	5♠	6♣
dbl	all pass		

If North is 5-5 or better, he jumps to 2NT at his first turn. However, he is 6-4 so he overcalls the six-card suit. Later his 4NT implies this shape, and encourages South to support clubs, which he is happy to do. The five-level is the limit of the East-West hands, and 6♣ is a good sacrifice. West has to double and settle for 500 rather than 650.

Unusual-over-Unusual

Unusual-over-Unusual is the defense I like when the opponents make a two-suited bid like Michaels, 'top and other' or Unusual Notrump (UNT). Cuebids of the implied suits are forward-going (10+ points). The lower cuebid always shows hearts, and the upper cuebid always shows spades.

West	North	East	South
1♡	2NT	3♣[1]	
1♡	2NT	3◇[2]	

1. Hearts, 10+ points with heart support.
2. Spades, five-plus-card suit, game-forcing.

West	North	East	South
1♠	2NT	3♣[1]	
1♠	2NT	3◇[2]	

1. Hearts, five-plus-card suit, game forcing.
2. Spades, 10+ points with spade support.

Directly bidding the other major is non-forcing. A raise of partner's major to the three-level is just competitive showing a constructive raise (a really good 7 points, a good 8 points or any 9 points). A double is a pre-penalty double, and says that one of the opponent's suits can be doubled. Shortness in partner's suit and four or more trumps are needed for the double. All doubles are penalty after that, and partner must double anything he can.

A similar treatment (anti-Michaels) works over Michaels too:

West	North	East	South	
1♠	2♠	pass	0 to 8	
		3♠	7 to 9 with support	
		dbl	pre-penalty double	
		3♣	natural, invitational, 10 to 12	
		3◇	natural, invitational, 10 to 12	
		3♡	the only cuebid, 10+ with support	

In addition to a pre-penalty double, the double has two alternative treatments. It can tell partner it is safe to lead the suit because a high honor is held, or it can show a simple raise (stolen bid). I prefer the penalty-oriented double showing either 4-4 or better in the two possible unspecified suits or four or more hearts.

Sandwich Notrump

West	North	East	South
1♠	2NT	pass	3NT
all pass			

Once I was sitting East, and I heard the above auction. By the second or third trick, I had figured out that East was not 5-5 in the minors. He had 20-21 and a spade stopper. That is not Unusual, but is really unusual. It is also quite a waste of a bid that will only occur once in a blue moon. It is more practical and frequent for a jump to 2NT over 1♠ to be used as unusual for the minors. Now consider the following auction.

West	North	East	South
1♣	pass	1♠	1NT
all pass			

Some play this as 15-18 with a stopper in both black suits. This is actually a dangerous situation because South could end up playing 1NT doubled with zero entries in dummy. A better and more frequent use of this bid is called Sandwich. It shows the unbid suits and 8-11 HCP. A contract is a little easier to play when not all of the available points are in declarer's hand. You should be 5-4 not vulnerable and 5-5 vulnerable. So the requirements are less strict than UNT, but you are also going to play at a lower level if you buy the hand.

Example 8.23 Two Bids in One

Neither vul.

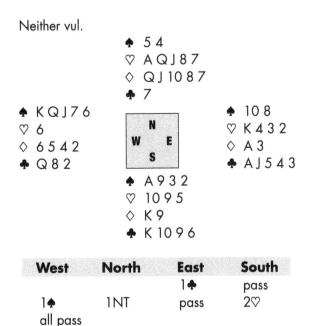

West	North	East	South
		1♣	pass
1♠	1NT	pass	2♡
all pass			

The Sandwich 1NT is much safer for North than a 2♡ overcall into a live auction, and also doesn't promise huge values. Here South ends up in a good contract.

Leaping Michaels

This convention is specifically used for big two-suiters over preemptive openings. The following five examples show very strong two-suited hands.

West	North	East	South
		2◇	4◇[1]

1. Five hearts and five spades.

West	North	East	South
		2♡	4♣[1]

1. Five spades and five clubs.

West	North	East	South
		2♡	4◇[1]

1. Five spades and five diamonds.

West	North	East	South
		2♠	4♣[1]

1. Five hearts and five clubs.

West	North	East	South
		2♠	4◇[1]

1. Five hearts and five diamonds.

Example 8.24 Leaping To Success

Neither vul.

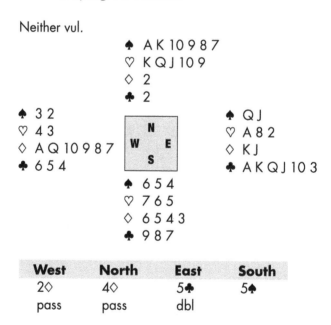

	♠ A K 10 9 8 7
	♡ K Q J 10 9
	◇ 2
	♣ 2

♠ 3 2   ♠ Q J
♡ 4 3   ♡ A 8 2
◇ A Q 10 9 8 7 ◇ K J
♣ 6 5 4   ♣ A K Q J 10 3

        ♠ 6 5 4
        ♡ 7 6 5
        ◇ 6 5 4 3
        ♣ 9 8 7

West	North	East	South
2◇	4◇	5♣	5♠
pass	pass	dbl	

North's 4◇ shows the majors. For East-West, 5♣ and 5◇ make, so 5♠ is a sacrifice as it turns out. There is a bit of guesswork at the five-level, and South is taking out insurance by not defending 5♣. His 5♠ will go down one for -100, which is better than the -400 alternative. Those playing 'top and other' usually play Michaels at high levels (or they should).

What are These Bids?

Here are some cuebids you should discuss with your partner:

a.

West	North	East	South
		1♣	3♣[1]

1. Preempt? Opening hand with 6+ clubs? Asking for notrump stopper? (My choice.)

b.

West	North	East	South
		1♡	3♡[1]

1. Asking for notrump stopper.

c.

West	North	East	South
		2◇	3◇[1]

1. Michaels? Asking for notrump stopper if Leaping Michaels is used?

d.

West	North	East	South
		2♡	3♡[1]

1. Michaels? Asking for notrump stopper if Leaping Michaels is used?

e.

West	North	East	South
1♣	pass	1♠	pass
1NT	2♣[1]		

1. Natural.

f.

West	North	East	South
1♣	pass	1♠	2♠[1]

1. Natural.

g.

West	North	East	South
1♡	pass	1♠	2♡[1]

1. Is this Michaels, with 2NT available to show minors?

h.

West	North	East	South
1♣	pass	1♠	2♣[1]

1. Natural.

And watch out for these related auctions:

i.

West	North	East	South
pass	pass	pass	1♠
1NT[1]			

1. Two lower unbid.

j.

West	North	East	South
1♡	pass	pass	2NT[1]

1. Natural, 20-21 HCP.

Two-suited hands lead very nicely to competitive situations. It is important to play Unusual-over-Unusual and have an understanding of what the bids in this section mean.

Chapter Nine

Sometimes Your Bids Help the Opposition

What is the downside of preempting, or competing at all, with wasted honors? Honors in your short suits may fall under the opponents' high cards. Then what can happen is that the opponents who, when in doubt, tend to bid on, find themselves in a thin game that comes home on a lucky distribution. In competitive auctions, good players bid on when in doubt. Don't push them into something that they wouldn't have reached on their own, when you know the cards are lying well for them.

Example 9.1 Sometimes Preempts Help

This deal came up during a pairs event at a Summerland, BC sectional.

Neither vul.

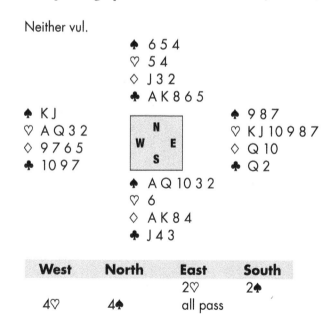

♠ 6 5 4
♥ 5 4
♦ J 3 2
♣ A K 8 6 5

♠ K J
♥ A Q 3 2
♦ 9 7 6 5
♣ 10 9 7

♠ 9 8 7
♥ K J 10 9 8 7
♦ Q 10
♣ Q 2

♠ A Q 10 3 2
♥ 6
♦ A K 8 4
♣ J 4 3

West	North	East	South
		2♥	2♠
4♥	4♠	all pass	

I am not saying East should pass, but if East-West do stay out, North-South are very likely to stop in partscore. Because of the preempt with 4 points in wasted honors and West's four-card support, North-South are forced to bid a making game, which in an uncontested auction, they will never reach. West used the Law of Total Tricks and foolishly thought he could keep North out of the bidding. At matchpoints, when in doubt, do not stretch to a marginal game. However, over an adverse preempt, do stretch to bid because otherwise you will be stolen blind.

Example 9.2   When in Doubt, Bid

Neither vul.

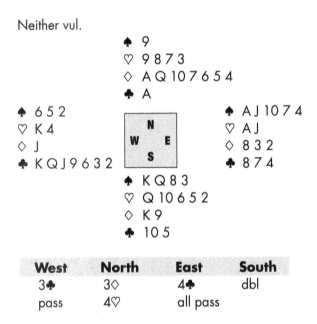

West	North	East	South
3♣	3◊	4♣	dbl
pass	4♡	all pass	

North-South reach game on momentum after the preempt; they may not do so without it. Yes, 4♡ can be beaten, but it takes very precise defense to do so (West must lead a diamond, win the first round of trumps with the king, lead a spade to his partner's ace, and ruff a diamond with the ♡4).

Example 9.3 Sometimes Preempts Show Partner Has Little Wasted

N-S vul.

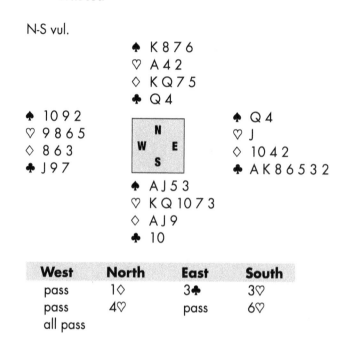

♠ K 8 7 6
♡ A 4 2
◇ K Q 7 5
♣ Q 4

♠ 10 9 2
♡ 9 8 6 5
◇ 8 6 3
♣ J 9 7

♠ Q 4
♡ J
◇ 10 4 2
♣ A K 8 6 5 3 2

♠ A J 5 3
♡ K Q 10 7 3
◇ A J 9
♣ 10

West	North	East	South
pass	1◇	3♣	3♡
pass	4♡	pass	6♡
all pass			

This deal was played in a KO teams at a Victoria regional tournament. Here again the preempt helped, by showing that North likely did not have a lot of wasted club values. Therefore, with his singleton club, South jumped to 6♡. He could not get the spades wrong in the play!

Example 9.4 Why Push Opponents to Game?

This deal occurred during an ACBL IMP speedball tourney on BBO. North-South were pushed to the correct spot.

Both vul.

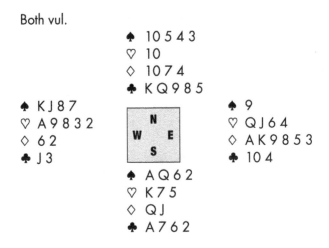

```
              ♠ 10 5 4 3
              ♡ 10
              ◇ 10 7 4
              ♣ K Q 9 8 5
♠ K J 8 7                        ♠ 9
♡ A 9 8 3 2        N             ♡ Q J 6 4
◇ 6 2          W       E         ◇ A K 9 8 5 3
♣ J 3              S             ♣ 10 4
              ♠ A Q 6 2
              ♡ K 7 5
              ◇ Q J
              ♣ A 7 6 2
```

West	North	East	South
pass	pass	1◇	1NT
2♡	dbl[1]	3♡	3♠
4♡	4♠	pass	pass
dbl	all pass		

1. Negative.

The sad part of this auction is that if South passes, 3♡ will likely be passed out. West cannot say any more. West suspects his spade honors are in the right place, but still really cannot justify taking another bid. South's wasted diamond honors should suggest selling out to 3♡, and indeed, 4♡ cannot be beaten.

PART 3

HIGH-LEVEL COMPETITION

Chapter Ten

Sacrifices

A successful sacrifice is any contract that goes down and gives the opponents a worse score than they can get playing their own contract. Common sacrifices, in competitive auctions, are going down two not vulnerable and down one vulnerable. These contracts, like most sacrifices, must be doubled to maximize the penalty.

Here are my rules for sacrifices:

- Unilateral sacrifices are not usually made.
- The sacrifice suit is not partner's shortest suit.
- Double fits lead to stellar sacrifices.
- There should be shortness, not honors, in any opponent's suit.
- There must be few or no defensive tricks. Too much defense leads to a phantom sacrifice made over a contract that was going to fail.

Example 10.1 Unilateral Action is Often Bad

Neither vul.

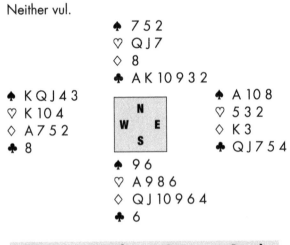

	♠ 752	
	♡ QJ7	
	◇ 8	
	♣ AK10932	

♠ KQJ43		♠ A108
♡ K104		♡ 532
◇ A752		◇ K3
♣ 8		♣ QJ754

	♠ 96	
	♡ A986	
	◇ QJ10964	
	♣ 6	

West	North	East	South
1♠	pass	2♠	pass
3♠	pass	4♠	5◇
dbl	all pass		

South's 5◇ doubled went down three for -500 and -7.2 IMPs. It was a phantom sacrifice, and he got what he deserved. But both players were at fault here, as North should overcall 2♣. That would tell South to stay out of the auction because of his stiff club, and a sacrifice would wait for another deal. Equal vulnerability sacrifices are not as common as favorable vulnerability sacrifices and are more common than unfavorable sacrifices. *When in doubt, do not sacrifice at all, but especially at equal vulnerability or worse.*

Example 10.2 Finding a Double Fit

E-W vul.

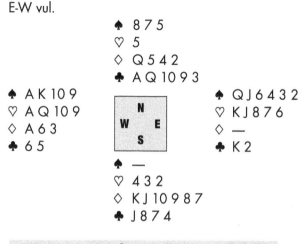

```
                    ♠ 8 7 5
                    ♡ 5
                    ◇ Q 5 4 2
                    ♣ A Q 10 9 3
♠ A K 10 9                        ♠ Q J 6 4 3 2
♡ A Q 10 9        N              ♡ K J 8 7 6
◇ A 6 3        W     E           ◇ —
♣ 6 5             S              ♣ K 2
                    ♠ —
                    ♡ 4 3 2
                    ◇ K J 10 9 8 7
                    ♣ J 8 7 4
```

West	North	East	South
			2◇
dbl	5♣	5♠	6♣
6♠	7◇	pass	pass
dbl	all pass		

If you read this book and bid like North for a loss of 500, I'd like to play a hand or two with you sometime. Did I say that a preempt must not be made with a void? Yes, rules are meant to be broken especially when you are really weak and really short in the majors. West made an off-shape double, but he has an ace above a normal double of a weak two, and he is 4-4 in the majors. North's 5♣ was an excellent bid, taking away a lot of room including Blackwood and letting partner know what to lead. If 5♣ gets doubled, he bids 5◇ as he intended when partner opened 2◇. North's bid of 5♣ should always imply diamond tolerance. How can anybody think anything else?

East could bid 5◇ to show both majors, but since his spades are longer, he bids 5♠. When South bids 6♣, North knows they have a good double fit and can safely bid 7◇. Seven-level sacrifices often have double fits. This seven-level sacrifice is so successful that East-West do not even recoup the value of their game, not to mention the slam. Both North-South have zero defense outside of their ten-card and nine-card fits. The ten-card fit is the obvious choice because a defensive club ruff is slightly less likely than a defensive diamond ruff. Furthermore, they hold the ♣A and not the ◊A. In 7◊ doubled, a club ruff is less likely when the declaring side has the ♣A.

Example 10.3 Jump as High as You Can Right Away

This hand occurred during an ACBL matchpoint speedball tourney on BBO.

N-S vul.

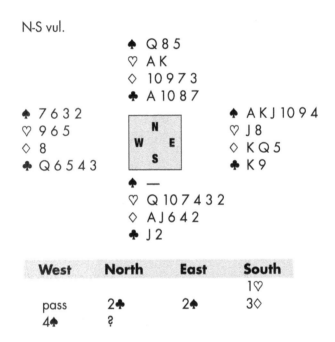

	♠ Q 8 5	
	♡ A K	
	◊ 10 9 7 3	
	♣ A 10 8 7	

♠ 7 6 3 2		♠ A K J 10 9 4
♡ 9 6 5		♡ J 8
◊ 8		◊ K Q 5
♣ Q 6 5 4 3		♣ K 9

	♠ —	
	♡ Q 10 7 4 3 2	
	◊ A J 6 4 2	
	♣ J 2	

West	North	East	South
			1♡
pass	2♣	2♠	3◊
4♠	?		

South is a little light for his 1♡ opening. However, he is stretching the Rule of 20, because he recognizes the value of a 6-5 hand.

You should always give the opponents the last guess and minimize the information they can exchange. West does well to jump to 4♠ and not wait to see whether the opponents get to game. If he is unsure, he must pass and avoid pushing them there. North is more likely to bid 5◊ than 5♡, and East-West will get a very good result compared to those pairs defending a heart contract. This is the most basic type of sacrifice, holding the higher-ranking suit. Here, 4♠ doubled would be down one for -100, if East-West were so fortunate as to get to play it there.

Example 10.4 Reach for the Stars

A similar deal occurred during an ACBL matchpoint speedball tourney on BBO.

N-S vul.

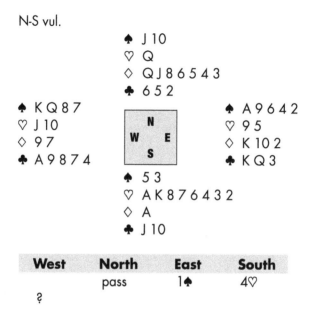

```
                    ♠ J 10
                    ♡ Q
                    ◇ Q J 8 6 5 4 3
                    ♣ 6 5 2
  ♠ K Q 8 7                          ♠ A 9 6 4 2
  ♡ J 10                             ♡ 9 5
  ◇ 9 7                              ◇ K 10 2
  ♣ A 9 8 7 4                        ♣ K Q 3
                    ♠ 5 3
                    ♡ A K 8 7 6 4 3 2
                    ◇ A
                    ♣ J 10
```

West	North	East	South
	pass	1♠	4♡
?			

West will be forced to show support by bidding 4♠ and then North-South get a plus score because 4♠ is down one. The best East-West can do, however, is to defend 4♡ doubled, but it is an impossible contract to reach. West's double probably should be negative up to 4♡, but even if it is not, finding a penalty double with four spades is still difficult.

Example 10.5 Nice Six-level Sacrifice

E-W vul.

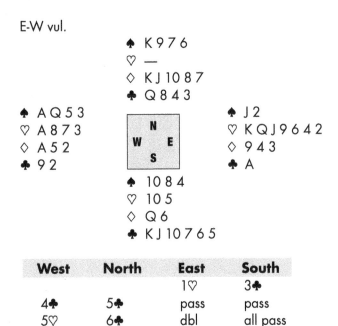

```
                    ♠ K 9 7 6
                    ♡ —
                    ◊ K J 10 8 7
                    ♣ Q 8 4 3
  ♠ A Q 5 3              N              ♠ J 2
  ♡ A 8 7 3          W       E          ♡ K Q J 9 6 4 2
  ◊ A 5 2                S              ◊ 9 4 3
  ♣ 9 2                                 ♣ A
                    ♠ 10 8 4
                    ♡ 10 5
                    ◊ Q 6
                    ♣ K J 10 7 6 5
```

West	North	East	South
		1♡	3♣
4♣	5♣	pass	pass
5♡	6♣	dbl	all pass

This deal occurred during the team event of a Moses Lake sectional, in Washington State. First of all, should East open at the one-level? He makes game if West has the ♡10 and ◊AKQ and various other sub-openers. Yes, East has an opening bid. Secondly, whoever said not to sacrifice at teams is quite wrong. Here is a perfect example of when to sacrifice. (Even an unlikely diamond lead doesn't beat 5♡, as declarer can strip the hand and endplay North.) North has a useful void and some defense against a slam, so he isn't worried about pushing them to 6♡.

Example 10.6 Sacrifices Really Do Work at Teams

Neither vul.

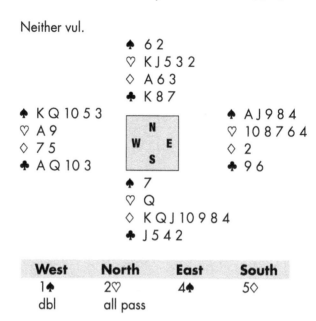

	♠ 6 2
	♡ K J 5 3 2
	◇ A 6 3
	♣ K 8 7

♠ K Q 10 5 3   ♠ A J 9 8 4
♡ A 9   ♡ 10 8 7 6 4
◇ 7 5   ◇ 2
♣ A Q 10 3   ♣ 9 6

                      ♠ 7
                      ♡ Q
                      ◇ K Q J 10 9 8 4
                      ♣ J 5 4 2

West	North	East	South
1♠	2♡	4♠	5◇
dbl	all pass		

This deal occurred during a local team game. South has an ideal hand with little defense and two-suited in the minors. Singleton queens win few tricks, so South hopes that North does not have four defensive tricks or three with diamond shortness. North-South conceded +100 in 5◇ doubled down one but gained 8 IMPs because 4♠ made at the other table.

Example 10.7 Equal Vulnerability Sacrifices Are Risky

Both vul.

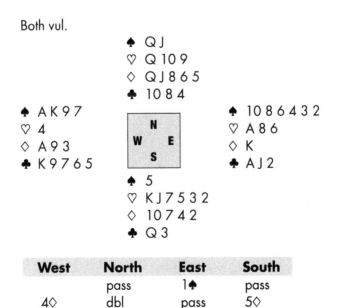

	♠ Q J	
	♡ Q 10 9	
	◊ Q J 8 6 5	
	♣ 10 8 4	

West	North	East	South
	pass	1♠	pass
4◊	dbl	pass	5◊
dbl	all pass		

This hand occurred in an ACBL BBO matchpoint speedball tourney. East-West have a grand, and out of thirty-nine tables, two were in a grand, and eight were in a small slam. Losing 1100 was a bad sacrifice because not enough pairs were in slam. The defenders, who might not even have reached slam, beat everybody in game with their +1100.

West, of course, meant to make a 4♡ splinter, and 4◊ was a mis-click. (West is really much too strong to splinter.) This *faux pas* gave North a chance to double, not for the lead but to suggest a possible sacrifice. (There is no future in leading a suit in which the declaring side has shortness and it may even set up discards for the declarer.) However, North showed poor judgment: the wasted spade and club honors argue against there being a good sacrifice, and he has the flattest possible hand that includes a five-card suit.

Example 10.8 Unfavorable Vulnerability Sacrifices Are Extremely Risky

N-S vul.

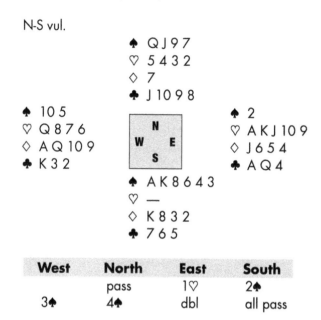

```
              ♠ Q J 9 7
              ♡ 5 4 3 2
              ◇ 7
              ♣ J 10 9 8
  ♠ 10 5                      ♠ 2
  ♡ Q 8 7 6        N          ♡ A K J 10 9
  ◇ A Q 10 9    W     E       ◇ J 6 5 4
  ♣ K 3 2          S          ♣ A Q 4
              ♠ A K 8 6 4 3
              ♡ —
              ◇ K 8 3 2
              ♣ 7 6 5
```

West	North	East	South
	pass	1♡	2♠
3♠	4♠	dbl	all pass

To the utter chagrin of East-West, 4♠ doubled is only down one for +200 while 5♡ makes six because the diamond king is onside. East-West were actually licking their lips as the bidding ended, in anticipation of a juicy 500 or more against their own not-vulnerable game. South's bidding, based on 6-4-3-0 distribution, no wasted honors and strength in the long suits, leads to North making a good sacrifice. South does have a possible defensive trick in diamonds and maybe one in spades, but it turns out there is only one actual defensive trick. An adverse vulnerability sacrifice almost never pays off. Those who do make them are usually having a bad game and are trying to kick-start a comeback — or perhaps they are having a bad game because they ignore vulnerability.

Example 10.9 Go Slowly to Make Them Sacrifice

This was a deal that occurred during the semifinals of a KO teams at the Victoria regional tournament. Here one of the players chose a certain bid because he *wanted* the opponents to take a save.

Both vul.

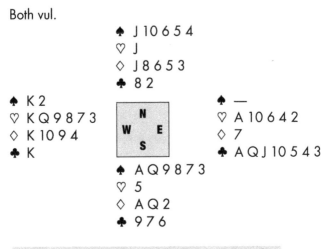

♠ J 10 6 5 4
♡ J
◇ J 8 6 5 3
♣ 8 2

♠ K 2
♡ K Q 9 8 7 3
◇ K 10 9 4
♣ K

♠ —
♡ A 10 6 4 2
◇ 7
♣ A Q J 10 5 4 3

♠ A Q 9 8 7 3
♡ 5
◇ A Q 2
♣ 9 7 6

West	North	East	South
		1♣	2♠
3♡	4♠	4NT	pass
5♣	pass	6♡	pass
pass	6♠	dbl	all pass

Of course, East could simply have jumped to 6♡ once he knew about the heart fit. However, they might not sacrifice if East jumps, and East wanted them to sacrifice for two reasons: suits are not likely to be breaking, and he doesn't know who has the ♣K (and has no real way to find out). If he can talk them into bidding 6♠, he has a sure plus. A slam that is bid methodically is much more likely to succeed than a slam bid with a jump and lack of information, so a sacrifice may work out well. A slam that is jumped to could be a flyer. Against such a slam, you should not sacrifice, and on defense, you should make an aggressive lead.

Example 10.10 Take Out Insurance

The following hand occurred during a Swiss event at a Vernon sectional. It was amazing that East-West, with a good spade fit, allowed the opponents to play 4♡, especially when they were not vulnerable. Bidding 4♠ not vulnerable is taking out a worthwhile bridge insurance policy and should have been done right away.

N-S vul.

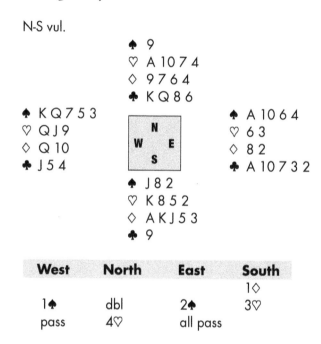

West	North	East	South
			1◇
1♠	dbl	2♠	3♡
pass	4♡	all pass	

North-South got +620 for 4♡ making and lost 300 for 4♠ doubled down two at the other table, for a gain of 8 IMPs. It makes things very interesting if East obeys the Law and bids 3◇ not 2♠. This jump cuebid shows a mixed raise, a very useful descriptive bid. It shows four-card support and fewer than ten points. It is a mixture of a preemptive bid and a single raise.

Example 10.11 South Did the Beginner Thing

E-W vul.

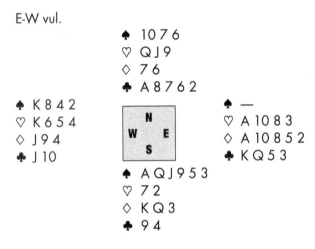

	♠ 10 7 6	
	♡ Q J 9	
	◇ 7 6	
	♣ A 8 7 6 2	
♠ K 8 4 2		♠ —
♡ K 6 5 4	N	♡ A 10 8 3
◇ J 9 4	W E	◇ A 10 8 5 2
♣ J 10	S	♣ K Q 5 3
	♠ A Q J 9 5 3	
	♡ 7 2	
	◇ K Q 3	
	♣ 9 4	

West	North	East	South
		1◇	1♠
dbl	2♣	3♡	pass??
4♡	pass	pass	4♠
pass	pass	dbl	all pass

This deal occurred during the semifinals of the KO teams at a Victoria regional tournament. By this point in the book, you know that if South is going to bid 4♠, he needs to do it right away over 3♡. This gives the opponents the last guess. Here they have settled in their contract, and then each of them in turn has the chance to express an opinion on bidding on or doubling. Here 4♠ is a phantom, but an immediate 4♠ might have persuaded one of them to bid 5♡.

Example 10.12 A Unilateral Phantom

Both vul.

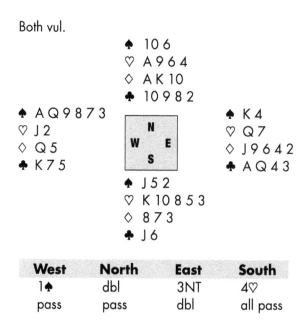

```
                    ♠ 10 6
                    ♡ A 9 6 4
                    ◇ A K 10
                    ♣ 10 9 8 2
  ♠ A Q 9 8 7 3                      ♠ K 4
  ♡ J 2            N                 ♡ Q 7
  ◇ Q 5         W     E              ◇ J 9 6 4 2
  ♣ K 7 5          S                 ♣ A Q 4 3
                    ♠ J 5 2
                    ♡ K 10 8 5 3
                    ◇ 8 7 3
                    ♣ J 6
```

West	North	East	South
1♠	dbl	3NT	4♡
pass	pass	dbl	all pass

This hand occurred during an ACBL BBO speedball tourney. South was in 4♡ doubled down two for a loss of 500. Over twenty-five tables, this was the third-worst score. Only at nine tables did East-West get a plus score, and most of those pairs were in a spade partscore making +140. South had no defense outside the heart suit but they can take five heart tricks and two top diamonds for +300 against 3NT. North had a light double but not every opening hand has three quick tricks, and not every takeout double will deliver four-card heart support.

Example 10.13 Sacrificing with Aces Can Be Ill-advised

Neither vul.

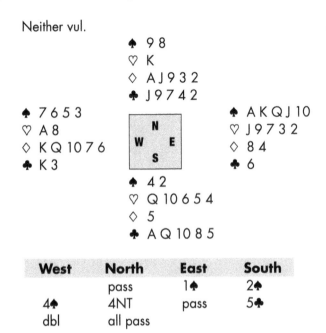

♠ 9 8
♡ K
◇ A J 9 3 2
♣ J 9 7 4 2

♠ 7 6 5 3
♡ A 8
◇ K Q 10 7 6
♣ K 3

♠ A K Q J 10
♡ J 9 7 3 2
◇ 8 4
♣ 6

♠ 4 2
♡ Q 10 6 5 4
◇ 5
♣ A Q 10 8 5

West	North	East	South
	pass	1♠	2♠
4♠	4NT	pass	5♣
dbl	all pass		

This deal came up in an ACBL matchpoint speedball tourney on BBO. This was a phantom sacrifice because of the ◇A and a ruff. North hoped that his partner did not have a singleton diamond (even though South is known to have at least ten cards in the rounded suits) but could have chosen not to sacrifice because of a poor secondary fit. *Sacrificing with good fits and double fits is advised, while sacrificing with aces, adverse honors and wasted honors is ill-advised.*

Example 10.14 Recognize When Opponents Are in Trouble

This hand was played during an ACBL IMP speedball tourney on BBO. The key to competitive bidding is to figure out the optimum contracts, which are 3♡ by South or 3♣ by East. Therefore, North-South deserve a positive on this board.

E-W vul.

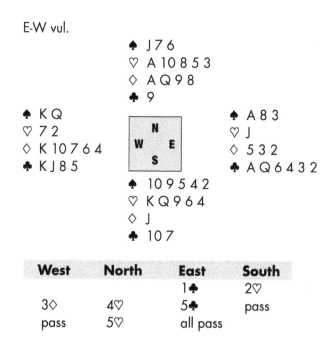

West	North	East	South
		1♣	2♡
3◊	4♡	5♣	pass
pass	5♡	all pass	

North would have received a gift of 500 if he had doubled 5♣, but he did not realize it, and turned a decent plus into a minus by bidding on. Part of the problem was South saying he had a weak two in hearts, but that should not have mattered because 5♣ was still in trouble. However, it is never optimum to represent a two-suited hand as one-suited. Furthermore, North did not listen to the bidding. West likely has the ◊K, so the ◊A and ◊Q are bigger assets on defense than on offense especially if South has a singleton. North should raise to 3♡ and then start doubling.

Example 10.15 Stretching When Vulnerable Can Be Hazardous

Both vul.

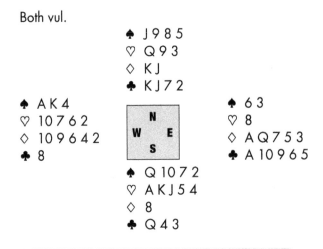

```
              ♠ J 9 8 5
              ♡ Q 9 3
              ◊ K J
              ♣ K J 7 2

♠ A K 4                          ♠ 6 3
♡ 10 7 6 2          N            ♡ 8
◊ 10 9 6 4 2    W       E        ◊ A Q 7 5 3
♣ 8                 S            ♣ A 10 9 6 5

              ♠ Q 10 7 2
              ♡ A K J 5 4
              ◊ 8
              ♣ Q 4 3
```

West	North	East	South
	pass	1◊	1♡
2♡	3♡	5♣	5♡
dbl	all pass		

This hand occurred during a pairs game at a Trail summer sectional. South did not know what hit him. East wanted to play 5◊, but chose to make a lead-directing bid on the way. That worked out well as West knew his partner had the ♣A opposite his singleton. East even got a spade ruff with his singleton trump before the dust settled. The opponents got +1400 for 5♡ doubled down five and all the matchpoints. It is critical to realize when the opponents are out of their depth as East-West did here. At matchpoints, it is critical to push the opponents around and to know who has started to flounder at what point.

Chapter Eleven

High-Level Decisions

The three-level and the five-level are for the opponents. Sometimes it is a fight for the two-level. The opponents should never be allowed to play in their fit at the one- or two-level unless there is a bad split. In competitive auctions, the opponents will bid on when in doubt, so we do not push them to game unless we are sure they can be defeated.

DEFENSE AGAINST A SACRIFICE

Any time your side has bid game with full expectation of making it, and the opponents bid on, they must play doubled or not play at all. You should tend to prefer bidding a vulnerable game over an opponent's sacrifice if you think you can make it. If the player in direct seat has values in the opponent's suit, he doubles, otherwise he passes, and this pass is forcing. Essentially a pass says that the player has already shown his hand. The pass demands that partner either bid or double. No player takes the push unless he is certain the contract at the higher level will make. Otherwise, he doubles and takes whatever plus he can.

Example 11.1 Do East-West Take the Push?

E-W vul.

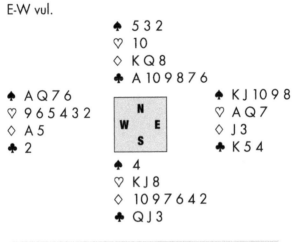

```
              ♠ 5 3 2
              ♡ 10
              ◇ K Q 8
              ♣ A 10 9 8 7 6
♠ A Q 7 6                      ♠ K J 10 9 8
♡ 9 6 5 4 3 2      N          ♡ A Q 7
◇ A 5           W     E       ◇ J 3
♣ 2                S          ♣ K 5 4
              ♠ 4
              ♡ K J 8
              ◇ 10 9 7 6 4 2
              ♣ Q J 3
```

West	North	East	South
		1♠	pass
4♣	dbl	pass	5♣
pass	pass	dbl	all pass

Here, 4♣ is a splinter in support of spades. Doubles of artificial bids are usually lead-directing. However, is North actually wanting the lead in a suit that there can be at most one trick for the defense? No, of course not. North has long clubs and little outside defense and is suggesting a sacrifice.

In response to West's splinter, East should cuebid if he has no wasted club values even with a minimum. A redouble of 4♣ would guarantee first-round club control. Here, he can do neither. He has wasted club values and a minimum, so he passes, which will allow West to bid 4♠. East has nothing to add to the story that his 1♠ opening has already told. Furthermore, West would have kept the bidding lower with Jacoby 2NT if he had extra values. Therefore, he intends to bid 4♠ and no higher.

However, South has good club support and little outside defense so he makes a 5♣ sacrifice. Sacrifices are mostly taken at favorable vulnerability, which is the case here.

Neither East nor West can bid 5♠, so East doubles. East-West must only take the push to a higher level when that contract is almost certain to make. Therefore, they must be content with whatever 5♣ doubled yields. East-West get +300 instead of +620 (South leads the ◇10), which is a minor victory because 5♠ goes down one for -100.

Example 11.2 Involve Partner in the High-level Decision

Both vul.

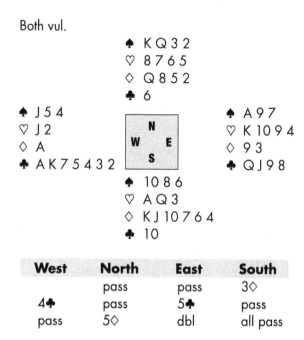

	♠ K Q 3 2	
	♡ 8 7 6 5	
	◇ Q 8 5 2	
	♣ 6	

♠ J 5 4		♠ A 9 7
♡ J 2		♡ K 10 9 4
◇ A		◇ 9 3
♣ A K 7 5 4 3 2		♣ Q J 9 8

	♠ 10 8 6	
	♡ A Q 3	
	◇ K J 10 7 6 4	
	♣ 10	

West	North	East	South
	pass	pass	3◇
4♣	pass	5♣	pass
pass	5◇	dbl	all pass

This is an example of what should not be done, from an ACBL matchpoint speedball tourney on BBO. North should involve South in the sacrifice decision. After all, a third-seat preempt can be pretty meaty, just not strong enough for game opposite a passed hand. It is an attempt at a shutout. It is normal to involve partner in decisions as much as possible, but it is even more important when partner makes a third-seat preempt. The bidding should go as follows.

West	North	East	South
	pass	pass	3◇
4♣	4◇	5♣	all pass

Example 11.3 Maximizing Profit

Essentially, the correct high-level decision has been made when profit has been maximized. I hope to make that maximization easier by example.

N-S vul.

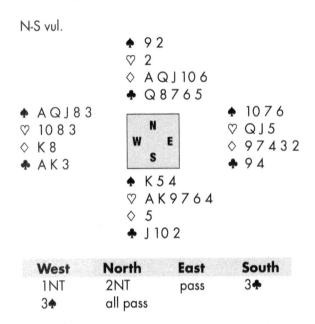

West	North	East	South
1NT	2NT	pass	3♣
3♠	all pass		

This deal was contested during an ACBL IMP speedball tourney on BBO. North bid 2NT over RHO's 1NT, showing the minors. North-South were playing modified DONT so he could have bid 2♣ showing clubs and a higher suit, but 2NT showed a decent 5-5 minor hand. North chose to enter the auction, so South must respect his decision and not introduce his heart suit. South bid 3♣ and then passed, refraining from stepping up the auction; he had decided to double 4♠ but doubling 3♠ seemed risky. As it turns out, 3♠ is only down one for +100, while 3♣ makes for +110. At IMPs, the board was a push. Meanwhile, only seven tricks are available in hearts.

Example 11.4 Do Not Think Lead Direction — Think Declaring

This was a deal that occurred in an ACBL speedball tourney on BBO.

E-W vul.

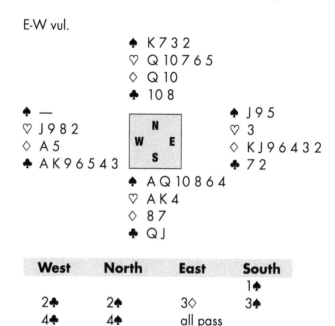

```
                 ♠ K 7 3 2
                 ♡ Q 10 7 6 5
                 ◇ Q 10
                 ♣ 10 8
   ♠ —                          ♠ J 9 5
   ♡ J 9 8 2          N         ♡ 3
   ◇ A 5         W         E    ◇ K J 9 6 4 3 2
   ♣ A K 9 6 5 4 3    S         ♣ 7 2
                 ♠ A Q 10 8 6 4
                 ♡ A K 4
                 ◇ 8 7
                 ♣ Q J
```

West	North	East	South
			1♠
2♣	2♠	3◇	3♠
4♣	4♠	all pass	

East put a lead-directing 3◇ bid in because he did not think he could get hurt with a seven-card suit opposite a 2♣ vulnerable overcall. And indeed, it pointed West to the correct switch once he had cashed the top two clubs. However, was 3◇ really lead-directing? No, that was West's slip. Yes, a bid by his partner at the three-level is always lead-directing, but partner also has club tolerance and an offense-oriented hand. West should bid 5♣, and indeed twelve tricks are available in clubs. Would partner have ventured a 3◇ bid with club shortness? No, that would be unwise.

Example 11.5 With a Fit in Hand, Experiment with Another

E-W vul.

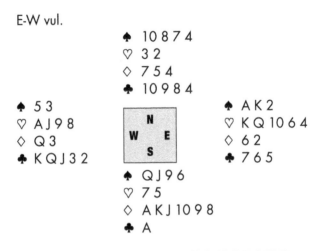

West	North	East	South
		1♡	2◇
3◇	4◇	4♡	4♠
pass	pass	dbl	all pass

West makes a cuebid showing a limit raise or better. North is competing strictly because the vulnerability is favorable. The Law of Total Tricks states that a nine-card fit is safe at the three-level, but the Law is not an absolute guide, and this is a good example of that. In this case, the double fit means that North-South are safe at the four-level. South knows North has nothing from the bidding, but expects four trumps opposite and refuses to let the opponents play game. He introduces his four-card spade suit because if partner does not have spade support, he can return to diamonds. North is fine with 5◇ doubled but is even happier a trick lower in 4♠ doubled. A double fit makes a sacrifice very profitable: East-West get +100 instead of +620. East certainly does not have extras, and neither does West, so bidding on cannot be a good option. The bidding does help South play the hand. It is safe to play for 2-2 diamonds because a singleton diamond might have persuaded East or West to bid 5♡.

Example 11.6 All the Way First Time

N-S vul.

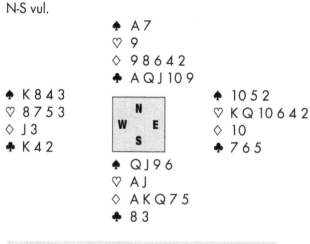

```
            ♠ A 7
            ♡ 9
            ◊ 9 8 6 4 2
            ♣ A Q J 10 9
♠ K 8 4 3                      ♠ 10 5 2
♡ 8 7 5 3         N            ♡ K Q 10 6 4 2
◊ J 3        W        E        ◊ 10
♣ K 4 2          S             ♣ 7 6 5
            ♠ Q J 9 6
            ♡ A J
            ◊ A K Q 7 5
            ♣ 8 3
```

West	North	East	South
		2♡	dbl
4♡	4NT	pass	5♡
pass	6♣	pass	6◊
all pass			

This deal occurred during the team event at a Moses Lake sectional. Here 4NT is not keycard: the trump suit has not been set so 4NT is asking partner to pick a minor. South's 5♡ shows first-round heart control and an insistence on a slam. North picks clubs, and South corrects to 6◊.

Competing with hearts over spades is not as easy as the reverse situation, but here West might have considered bidding 5♡ instead of 4♡. With a 7-count opposite a weak two-bid, he knows the opponents are on for at least a game, so despite his relatively flat shape, 5♡ is not a bad idea at this vulnerability. Here, if West had bid 5♡, North would have doubled for penalty and that would have been that.

Example 11.7 Pass and Pull

N-S vul.

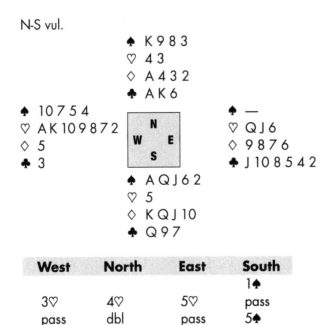

	♠ K 9 8 3	
	♡ 4 3	
	◇ A 4 3 2	
	♣ A K 6	
♠ 10 7 5 4		♠ —
♡ A K 10 9 8 7 2		♡ Q J 6
◇ 5		◇ 9 8 7 6
♣ 3		♣ J 10 8 5 4 2
	♠ A Q J 6 2	
	♡ 5	
	◇ K Q J 10	
	♣ Q 9 7	

West	North	East	South
			1♠
3♡	4♡	5♡	pass
pass	dbl	pass	5♠
pass	6♠	all pass	

When 5♡ comes around to North, he has a decision to bid or to double. North has a minimum opener, and does not have an extra king or ace to bid 5♠, therefore, he must double and take whatever plus he can get. Being in 5♠ down one would be a disaster if 5♡ doubled gave North-South a plus score. South passed 5♡ (a forcing pass), and then pulled partner's obligatory double. This tactic is called pass and pull — it shows heart shortness and slam interest. North can bid slam. Yes, if South does not have the ♠A, he will need a heart void, or the contract is going down. That's the way it is. There is no room for accurate bidding with an opponent preempting and his partner raising. However, here North-South earn 1430 for their successful slam.

Example 11.8 Accurate Bidding is Difficult in Preempted Auctions

Neither vul.

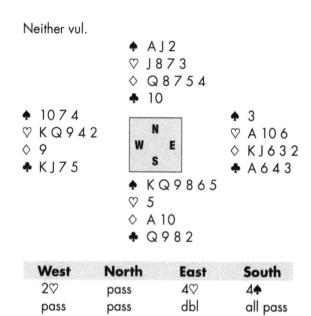

♠ A J 2
♥ J 8 7 3
♦ Q 8 7 5 4
♣ 10

♠ 10 7 4
♥ K Q 9 4 2
♦ 9
♣ K J 7 5

♠ 3
♥ A 10 6
♦ K J 6 3 2
♣ A 6 4 3

♠ K Q 9 8 6 5
♥ 5
♦ A 10
♣ Q 9 8 2

West	North	East	South
2♡	pass	4♡	4♠
pass	pass	dbl	all pass

This board was played thirty-six times in an ACBL IMP speedball tourney on BBO. You have to take chances in preempted auctions or there will be many instances of larceny. Here, 4♠ was bid a total of sixteen times, but was only doubled twice and defended properly only once. That particular West did the correct thing and led spades at his every opportunity. With best play, 4♠ is a phantom sacrifice because 4♡ does not make with proper defense.

Example 11.9 Being Void in the Opponent's Suit Can Be Good for Defense

This board came up in an ACBL IMP speedball tourney on BBO. It is an example of how a void in opponent's suit is a double-edged sword — they may not make their contract because of a bad split.

E-W vul.

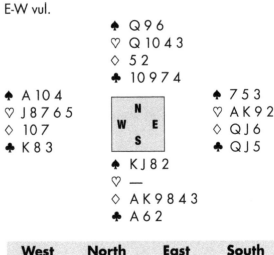

♠ Q 9 6
♥ Q 10 4 3
♦ 5 2
♣ 10 9 7 4

♠ A 10 4
♥ J 8 7 6 5
♦ 10 7
♣ K 8 3

♠ 7 5 3
♥ A K 9 2
♦ Q J 6
♣ Q J 5

♠ K J 8 2
♥ —
♦ A K 9 8 4 3
♣ A 6 2

West	North	East	South
pass	pass	1♡	dbl
4♡	pass	pass	5◇
all pass			

South was seduced by the vulnerability and his heart void into bidding on. At this vulnerability, he should be thinking of defending, especially since his partner may well have trump tricks. It works out better if South overcalls 2◇ and then doubles 4♡. Partner will be expected to pull it with lots of diamonds or a spade fit. Here 4♡ doubled goes down three, while 5◇ has no play.

Example 11.10 Watch Out for Tenuous Games

This happened in an ACBL BBO IMP speedball tourney.

Both vul.

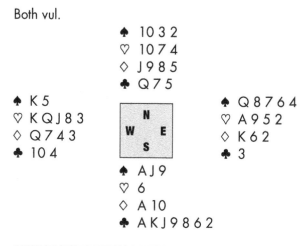

```
              ♠ 10 3 2
              ♡ 10 7 4
              ◇ J 9 8 5
              ♣ Q 7 5
♠ K 5                          ♠ Q 8 7 6 4
♡ K Q J 8 3         N          ♡ A 9 5 2
◇ Q 7 4 3       W     E        ◇ K 6 2
♣ 10 4              S          ♣ 3
              ♠ A J 9
              ♡ 6
              ◇ A 10
              ♣ A K J 9 8 6 2
```

West	North	East	South
			1♣
1♡	pass	2♣	3♣
4♡	pass	pass	5♣
pass	pass	dbl	all pass

South lost 200 in 5♣ doubled down one and would have had a good result for letting West play in 4♡ whether or not he doubled it. The final 5♣ was a bad unilateral bid made over a very dubious game. It cannot be forgotten how much people stretch at IMPs. Sacrifices at IMPs should be carefully judged so as not to give the opponents a plus score to which they are not entitled. (West can come to nine tricks as long as he guesses to play South for the doubleton ◇A — not hard on the auction.)

Example 11.11 Sacrificing Over a Minor-suit Game is Hard to Do

This happened during a Moses Lake sectional.

Both vul.

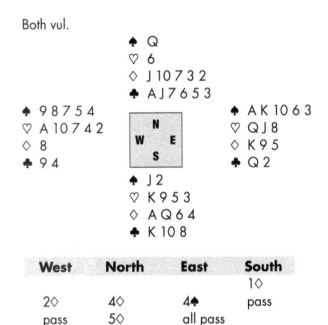

```
              ♠ Q
              ♡ 6
              ◇ J 10 7 3 2
              ♣ A J 7 6 5 3
  ♠ 9 8 7 5 4              ♠ A K 10 6 3
  ♡ A 10 7 4 2    N        ♡ Q J 8
  ◇ 8           W   E      ◇ K 9 5
  ♣ 9 4           S        ♣ Q 2
              ♠ J 2
              ♡ K 9 5 3
              ◇ A Q 6 4
              ♣ K 10 8
```

West	North	East	South
			1◇
2◇	4◇	4♠	pass
pass	5◇	all pass	

West made a pretty poor Michaels bid and paid for his mistake. In two-suited weak bids, both suits must be playable. The spade suit was not even close to being playable, and the hand was too weak, especially vulnerable. However, he got lucky with East's magnificent spade support. Unfortunately, 4♠ was not allowed to play because it makes, but it was doubly unfortunate that 5◇ was allowed to play. West bid more than he should have, so it was definitely up to East to sacrifice. With a double fit in the majors and the ◇K likely well-placed for the opponents, East must bid 5♠. Sacrificing over a minor-suit game often produces a bad result — you could push the opponents to a makeable slam, or you might find that the field was in 3NT and you were headed for a matchpoint good score. However, that is not the case here, where -100 was a good board, but -600 was a shared bottom.

Example 11.12 Bad Preempts Lead to Bad Results

This deal occurred during the team event of a Moses Lake sectional.

N-S vul.

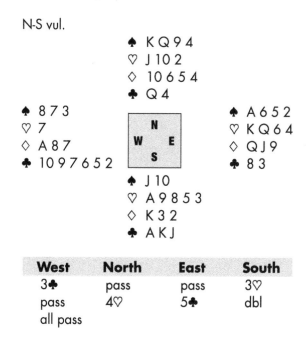

```
              ♠ K Q 9 4
              ♡ J 10 2
              ◇ 10 6 5 4
              ♣ Q 4
♠ 8 7 3                      ♠ A 6 5 2
♡ 7             N            ♡ K Q 6 4
◇ A 8 7      W     E         ◇ Q J 9
♣ 10 9 7 6 5 2   S          ♣ 8 3
              ♠ J 10
              ♡ A 9 8 5 3
              ◇ K 3 2
              ♣ A K J
```

West	North	East	South
3♣	pass	pass	3♡
pass	4♡	5♣	dbl
all pass			

Going back to my earlier theme, undisciplined preempts make it impossible for partner to judge the auction accurately. I held the West hand at the other table, and I never dreamed of introducing my club suit yet alone sacrificing in it. The opponents made a disastrous high-level decision that stemmed from a terrible preempt. Just stick to good sound bridge, and good results will follow. Here the preempt actually worked, in that North-South had got to a no-play game — but East completely misjudged the situation and decided to bid on. He was wrong in 800 ways.

Example 11.13 Vulnerability Helps in the Bid or Double Decision

Both vul.

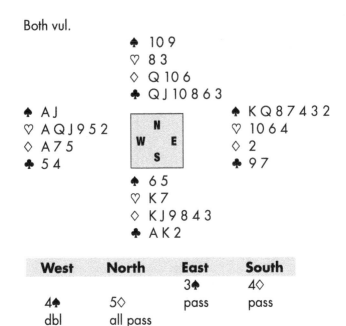

	♠ 10 9	
	♡ 8 3	
	◇ Q 10 6	
	♣ Q J 10 8 6 3	

♠ A J		♠ K Q 8 7 4 3 2
♡ A Q J 9 5 2		♡ 10 6 4
◇ A 7 5		◇ 2
♣ 5 4		♣ 9 7

	♠ 6 5	
	♡ K 7	
	◇ K J 9 8 4 3	
	♣ A K 2	

West	North	East	South
		3♠	4◇
4♠	5◇	pass	pass
dbl	all pass		

This board came up during an ACBL matchpoint speedball tourney on BBO. West had a problem: he could not bid 4♡ because he could be passed in an inferior contract with a spade fit all along. Therefore, he had to bid 4♠. He would have bid 5♡ over 5◇ if he were vulnerable against not vulnerable opponents, but at equal vulnerability, he decided to double. That got him 800. East-West will make +650 in either major on a club lead, or +710 if North leads a diamond against a heart contract.

Example 11.14 Open 2NT Whenever Possible

Sometimes low-level decisions, such as opening 2NT rather than one of a suit, are critical.

Both vul.

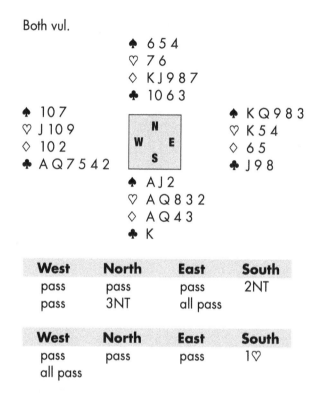

♠ 6 5 4
♥ 7 6
♦ K J 9 8 7
♣ 10 6 3

♠ 10 7
♥ J 10 9
♦ 10 2
♣ A Q 7 5 4 2

♠ K Q 9 8 3
♥ K 5 4
♦ 6 5
♣ J 9 8

♠ A J 2
♥ A Q 8 3 2
♦ A Q 4 3
♣ K

West	North	East	South
pass	pass	pass	2NT
pass	3NT	all pass	

West	North	East	South
pass	pass	pass	1♡
all pass			

South stretches to open 2NT because partner can have a hand, with 5 or a good 4 HCP, that passes a one-level opening but raises 2NT to 3NT. Furthermore, the flaw of the stiff king is not in a major, so it is not a double flaw. Here, 1♡ makes 170, and 3NT is 600. High-level decisions, in the long run, are made easier when 2NT is opened as often as possible.

Example 11.15 Doubling a Game Going Down Reaps Rewards

Neither vul.

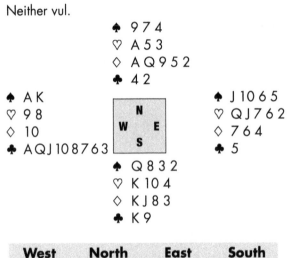

	♠ 9 7 4	
	♡ A 5 3	
	◇ A Q 9 5 2	
	♣ 4 2	
♠ A K		♠ J 10 6 5
♡ 9 8		♡ Q J 7 6 2
◇ 10		◇ 7 6 4
♣ A Q J 10 8 7 6 3		♣ 5
	♠ Q 8 3 2	
	♡ K 10 4	
	◇ K J 8 3	
	♣ K 9	

West	North	East	South
			1◇
2♣	3♣	pass	3NT
4♣	5◇	all pass	

This deal is from the KO teams at a Victoria regional tournament. First of all, South should bid 3◇ not 3NT because his club stopper really isn't good enough, and there is no obvious source of tricks. However, perhaps it bluffed West into not doubling 5◇. (The 3♣ cuebid shows 10+ and diamond support.) Secondly, West must double 5◇ and chalk up the 800 top to which he is entitled. Doubling a game that makes is not the end of the world, while doubling a partscore into game at IMPs is. That is not the case here. However, doubling a game that could go down two or more or is down one for sure is a must. At IMPs, doubling two of a minor is a similar situation: it may reap rewards, and the opponents are not being doubled into a game.

Chapter Twelve

Misfits

Misfits kill the ability to make as many tricks as your high-card holdings lead you to expect. The first person to discover the contract-crippling misfit bails and passes the auction out below game. Running to 3NT with a prayer is not a good idea. Yes, you see pairs blast away to 3NT, and perhaps make it because of leaky defense, but that is not good bridge. If partner is an aggressive bidder, it is even more critical to stop bidding when there is a misfit. It may help in the bidding to count a singleton in partner's five-card suit as minus three and a void as minus four. You must reevaluate and place the contract where it belongs.

Example 12.1 Bail and Do Not Run to 3NT

It is no secret that the best strategy to matchpoints is to get as many plus scores as possible. This means marginal games should not be bid at any vulnerability. Therefore, I get into the bidding every time I can. I open two-suited hands, that are 5-4 or better, using the modified Rule of 20 (the Rule of 20 with no wasted values). This means partner must not force to 3NT contracts in the face of a misfit. Misfit situations should cause one of the partners to bail.

N-S vul.

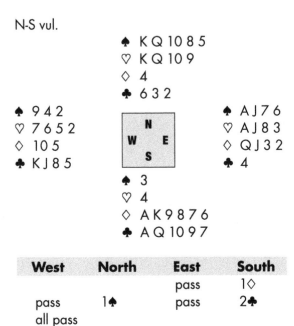

		♠ K Q 10 8 5	
		♡ K Q 10 9	
		◊ 4	
		♣ 6 3 2	

♠ 9 4 2		♠ A J 7 6
♡ 7 6 5 2		♡ A J 8 3
◊ 10 5		◊ Q J 3 2
♣ K J 8 5		♣ 4

		♠ 3	
		♡ 4	
		◊ A K 9 8 7 6	
		♣ A Q 10 9 7	

West	North	East	South
		pass	1◊
pass	1♠	pass	2♣
all pass			

North-South get +110 for 2♣ making plus one. Should North push on to game because an opener opposite an opener makes game? No, of course not. Even notrump contracts need things like a source of tricks and transportation. Can you see how difficult 3NT is? Declarer will have to work pretty hard to get even seven tricks. Players should not get into the habit of blasting to 3NT and blaming partner's hand for their own bidding shortcomings.

Example 12.2 Trumps Give the Weak Hand Entries

This deal occurred during the team event of a Moses Lake sectional.

Neither vul.

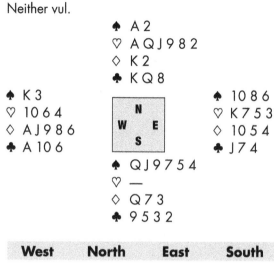

```
              ♠ A 2
              ♡ A Q J 9 8 2
              ◇ K 2
              ♣ K Q 8
♠ K 3                          ♠ 10 8 6
♡ 10 6 4                       ♡ K 7 5 3
◇ A J 9 8 6                    ◇ 10 5 4
♣ A 10 6                       ♣ J 7 4
              ♠ Q J 9 7 5 4
              ♡ —
              ◇ Q 7 3
              ♣ 9 5 3 2
```

West	North	East	South
		pass	pass
1◇	dbl	pass	2♠
pass	4♡	pass	4♠
all pass			

It's usually important to play a misfit in the weaker hand's long suit so the weak hand has entries. It was a bonus here for South to discover that partner had two spades. South made 4♠ plus one for +450. At the other table, the bidding went as follows, with West opening a 10-12 notrump, with North-South playing transfers as a defense.

West	North	East	South
		pass	pass
1NT	2◇*	pass	2♡
pass	4♡	all pass	

Perhaps South should have refused the transfer and bid 2♠. However, they played in 4♡ down one.

Example 12.3 With Length in the Opponent's Suit, Pass

N-S vul.

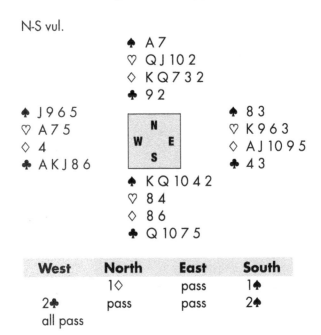

	♠ A 7		
	♡ Q J 10 2		
	◇ K Q 7 3 2		
	♣ 9 2		

West	North	East	South
	1◇	pass	1♠
2♣	pass	pass	2♠
all pass			

This was a deal that occurred in an ACBL matchpoint speedball tourney on BBO. When 2♣ comes around to South, he should realize that his partner did nothing even though he could be looking at club shortness. Therefore, South made a bad bid in face of a misfit. A loss of 200 was a bad board and -90 for 2♣ making would have been a good board. It is important to recognize how good fits and double fits work well, but it is also important to recognize misfits. South must defend 2♣ with four clubs.

Example 12.4 Good Habits Get Rewarded

Neither vul.

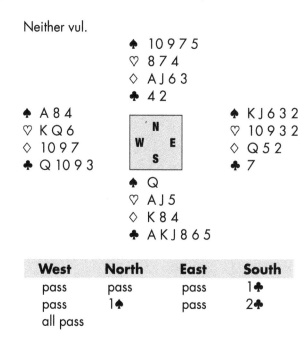

<pre>
                   ♠ 10 9 7 5
                   ♡ 8 7 4
                   ◇ A J 6 3
                   ♣ 4 2
     ♠ A 8 4   ♠ K J 6 3 2
     ♡ K Q 6   N   ♡ 10 9 3 2
     ◇ 10 9 7   W   E   ◇ Q 5 2
     ♣ Q 10 9 3   S   ♣ 7
                   ♠ Q
                   ♡ A J 5
                   ◇ K 8 4
                   ♣ A K J 8 6 5
</pre>

West	North	East	South
pass	pass	pass	1♣
pass	1♠	pass	2♣
all pass			

Here, after his partner bid his singleton, South dialed it back by rebidding only 2♣. A 2NT or 3NT response is wrong because of the spade holding. South should subtract 3 points for a singleton in partner's suit and that brings him down to 15 and a 2♣ rebid. South made 2♣ for +90, while on anything resembling defense, 2NT has no play.

Example 12.5 Stop Bidding Notrump with Shortness, Please

This deal was played in the main bridge room of BBO. This is a good example of how a misfit with North's longest suit kills prospects of slam.

N-S vul.

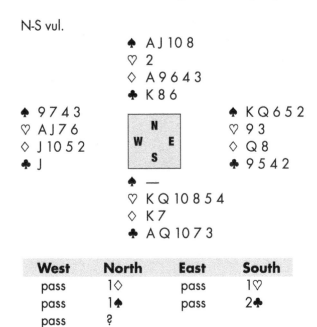

```
              ♠ A J 10 8
              ♡ 2
              ◇ A 9 6 4 3
              ♣ K 8 6

  ♠ 9 7 4 3              ♠ K Q 6 5 2
  ♡ A J 7 6              ♡ 9 3
  ◇ J 10 5 2            ◇ Q 8
  ♣ J                   ♣ 9 5 4 2

              ♠ —
              ♡ K Q 10 8 5 4
              ◇ K 7
              ♣ A Q 10 7 3
```

West	North	East	South
pass	1◇	pass	1♡
pass	1♠	pass	2♣
pass	?		

North bid 2NT now, and South assumed a doubleton heart opposite and pressed on to 6♡, which was not a success. Both players could be faulted here, though, because South did not allow his spade void to modify his enthusiasm once partner opened.

Example 12.6 The Weak Hand Decides

In example 12.2, the weak hand gets its long suit as trumps. This has been the basis of transfers over 1NT openings. The weak hand gets entries from having its suit as trumps and the strong hand remains hidden. This also applies when each partner has a long suit.

Both vul.

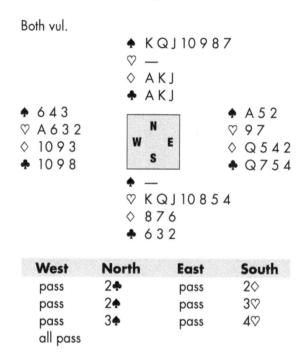

West	North	East	South
pass	2♣	pass	2◊
pass	2♠	pass	3♡
pass	3♠	pass	4♡
all pass			

There is no question there is a misfit, as North and South each have a void in partner's suit. The problem is solved by North, with game in his own hand, letting the weaker hand set hearts as trumps. There is no shortage of entries to the strong North hand, but there are no entries to the South hand unless hearts are trumps. Against good defense (finding exit cards), 4♠ makes +620, and 4♡ makes +680.

This example also solidifies the point of Example 4.11. When partner preempts, shortness in his suit does not mean you run to a 3NT contract unless you can count nine tricks without his suit. You need entries in the suit itself to make use of the preemptor's suit because he will have a good suit and a very limited amount of outside entries. When partner preempts or shows a weak hand with a long suit some other way, shortness in his suit is a warning to tread carefully. It will likely be better to play in his long suit, with or without support.

Example 12.7 But I Had Only One Diamond Loser

Neither vul.

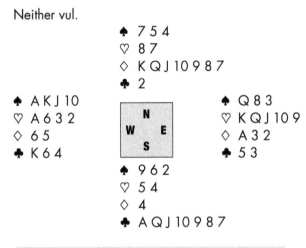

	♠ 7 5 4		
	♡ 8 7		
	◇ K Q J 10 9 8 7		
	♣ 2		

West	North	East	South
	3◇	pass	pass
dbl	pass	4♡	5♣
dbl	all pass		

When the dust settled, South had lost 1100. As I left the table, I heard him telling his partner, '... but I had only one diamond loser'.

So here's a player who did not take shortness in his partner's preempt suit as a dire warning to stay out of the auction. The singleton diamond should be a deal breaker — it's the reason that North's hand is useless as dummy. Playing clubs, North's diamond suit was never touched except to be discarded. It did not even matter that North had a good preempt.

Another serious problem was that a sacrifice in the club suit was unilateral. Partner should be involved in all high-level decisions, slams or sacrifices. Furthermore, South waited until the opponents essentially finished bidding. They had nothing more to say except double. While 5♣ is still a bad bid, it would show some bridge skill to make it right away and leave the opponents possibly wanting to say more than just double.

Let's change the hands keeping North and South still with the same 7-3-2-1 shape and East-West still making +450. East-West are playing takeout and negative doubles up to 7♡.

Neither vul.

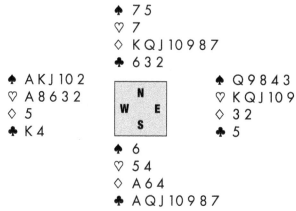

```
              ♠ 7 5
              ♡ 7
              ◇ K Q J 10 9 8 7
              ♣ 6 3 2
♠ A K J 10 2                    ♠ Q 9 8 4 3
♡ A 8 6 3 2        N           ♡ K Q J 10 9
◇ 5            W       E        ◇ 3 2
♣ K 4              S            ♣ 5
              ♠ 6
              ♡ 5 4
              ◇ A 6 4
              ♣ A Q J 10 9 8 7
```

What a contrast now that South has three diamonds. Now 6♣ or 6◇ goes down two for -300, which is much better than 5♡ or 5♠ making for +450. The double fit makes this an exception to needing favorable vulnerability for a worthwhile sacrifice. Indeed, at favorable vulnerability, double-fit situations may even lead to a successful seven-level sacrifice.

I gave South the ◇A here because we don't want to push the opponents to a successful slam. Without the ◇A, but the same shape, North-South just bid to the five-level, happy to take away as much room as possible, including Blackwood, and to keep a possible double fit hidden. Even without the ◇A in South's hand, 5◇ doubled is only -300 not -1100 in the initial layout. However, all is not lost for the South player on that deal, because the -1100 situation can be remedied with two doses — one of knowledge and one of patience.

Also New from Master Point Press

Hand of the Week

978-1-77140-028-2

Joel Martineau

Perhaps the best way to improve your bridge is to watch an expert play, and try to understand the reasoning behind their bids and plays. Here, readers follow the bidding and play (or defense) of fifty-two deals — one a week for a year — and listen to the author's thinking as each hand develops. Understanding why the experts do what they do is the first step towards being able to do it yourself — at least some of the time!

To Bid or Not To Bid
978-1-894154-48-2

Larry Cohen

Since its publication in 1992, *To Bid or Not to Bid* has sold over 50,000 copies in English alone and has been published in several other languages. Undoubtedly the best-selling bridge book of the 1990s, its lucid exposition of the empirical Law of Total Tricks (a simple guide to making the right decisions in competitive bridge auctions) has made it a book that literally every serious bridge player just has to read.

Brush Up Your Bidding

Improve Your Bidding Judgment
978-1-897106-29-7
Neil Kimelman

The Thin Fine Line
978-1-897106-93-8
Neil Kimelman

The Right Bid at the Right Time
978-1-77140-027-5
Neil Kimelman

In this three-book series, the author explores the basis of bidding judgment. In the modern game, most auctions are competitive; it is knowing when to take one more bid, and just as important, when not to, that separates the experts from the rest.